Please,
Daddy,
No

A BOY BETRAYED

Please,
Daddy,
No

STUART HOWARTH

WITH ANDREW CROFTS

HarperElement
An Imprint of HarperCollins*Publishers*
77–85 Fulham Palace Road
Hammersmith, London W6 8JB

The website address is: www.thorsonselement.com

and *HarperElement* are trademarks of
HarperCollins*Publishers* Limited

Published by HarperElement 2006

2

A catalogue record of this book is
available from the British Library

ISBN-13   978-0-00-723637-4
ISBN-10   0-00-723637-9

Printed and bound in Great Britain by
Clays Ltd, St Ives plc

This book is proudly printed on paper which contains wood
from well-managed forests, certified in accordance with
the rules of the Forest Stewardship Council.
For more information about FSC,
please visit www.fsc.org

Mixed Sources
Product group from well-managed
forests and other controlled sources
www.fsc.org Cert no. SW-COC-1806
© 1996 Forest Stewardship Council

FSC

TO MY SISTER
SHIRLEY ANNE HOWARTH

1 FEBRUARY 1965 – 8 FEBRUARY 1991
AGED 26 YEARS

I miss you, 'Shirl the Whirl',
and today I know that you escaped away
to peace and freedom.

I watch you dance in the summer meadows,
running free and chasing butterflies.

Today I smile for us all –
love you!

Acknowledgements

To my darling Tracey. You are my love, my life, my faith, my strength, my today, my tomorrow and my everlasting!

To Mum (thanks for keeping us together as a unit), Trevor, Christina, Clare, Rosina, Maria, Mark and Dominic. Now is the time to begin our journey as a family. To Sebastiano (God bless you) and to Eric (rest in peace).

To Matthew, Rebecca, Jamie and Lee. Thank you for teaching me how to be a father and for the warmth that engages me every time you are around. Thank you for my grandchildren and for the unconditional love they bring.

To Sue and Geoff Hadfield and the Hadfield family. You believed in me and showed much love where others would have turned their backs. I will always be grateful – thank you.

To my legal team: Padhee Singh, Ash Halam, Peter Pratt, Dr Keith Rix, Dr Lucinda Cochayne and the very honourable Mr Justice Elias.

To Colm O'Gorman (One in Four) – you heard my cries and felt my pain; Neil Fox (counsellor) – prison needed good men like you; the God Squad at Strangeways and the few officers who fought my cause (you know who you are), and the hundreds of men I came across in the prison system who shared their stories of abuse, hurt and pain with me (your anonymity remains as requested).

To Anthony Kelly (I followed the dream, thanks for the reviews); to Colin and Colleen Heath, the Taylors, Dean Mylchreest, Martin Cashin, the Sweeney Family, Jimmy Barlow (Do not fear, Uncle Jimmy is here), Vic Scantlebury, Del, Big Roy, Brett, Big Scott, Wints, Mark Brittain (big boys do cry), Scott Gledhill and Kerry Kayes (thanks for the support in prison), Colin and Leanne and the bike club, Roy Bailey, Roy Radcliffe, Tommy, Bob (oh yes), Derek, Big Steve, and all the Altrincham crew.

To Judy Chilcote and Andrew Crofts. Thanks for helping make this happen, for helping expose the truth and reality of this often cruel world.

To Richard and Helen McCann. Thanks for your unconditional support, encouragement, advice and assistance.

To Jim Browne (Fire in Ice Liverpool), Steve Bevan (Survivors Swindon), James Brett (your story must be told and I love you, man), Mike Lew (Victims no more) and Craig Charles (a brave and courageous man – expose the truth). To the thirty brave men I met recently on retreat who I saw reduced to small boys in pain and with tortured souls. You too can recover!

To Anthony Akka, my sponsor and trusted friend (direction and honesty) – you are an example to me; to Murad Mousa my pally, pal, pal and to Patrick Gallagher for your unreserved love. To Big Paul (up the Irish), the Prichards, Dennis, Daz Millington, Dave M., Mark, Dean (Scouse), Howard (Fireman Sam), Keith and Julie Clarke (MVS), Andy Banks, Steve Mather and Woody and Mike.

To all the staff at Altrincham Priory and again at Castle Craig (without you our souls would be lost forever); Wynn Parry, Jonathan, Richard, Bill, Ian, Eddy and Kevin – thank you. To the fellowships up and down the country who live their lives one day at a time and follow the righteous path!

To Ken and Kathryn. Your love for each other is amazing and you are in my thoughts and prayers on a daily basis. God bless you!

To the still suffering and survivors around the world. You are never alone. Feel no shame or guilt and break free from the horrors of the past. Expose your abuse and make the world listen.

To the families of those who suffer. Please forgive them and allow them to recover. Like a pebble dropped into a pond, the ripples run far and wide, and without recovery the symptoms pass on through generations.

Finally, to all those people that have been affected by my actions either directly or indirectly. I bow my head and offer my unreserved apologies.

Introduction

There are thousands of kids out there, just like me, who suffer abuse on a daily basis. You can turn a blind eye and consider this too nasty to read about, or you can take a courageous step forward and share a few moments from my world. We can only bring about change by doing something positive and being prepared to listen. This is my story.

Please,
Daddy,
No

Chapter One

DRIVING WEST

I know when I set out from Mum's pub that evening, 20 August 2000, I intended to go to pick up my girlfriend, Tracey, from her house. I know I intended to because otherwise I would never have taken the road I did. If I had set out with the intention of driving back to Wales I would have taken a more direct route.

Something happened inside my head between leaving Mum's and getting to Tracey's place, which stopped me from turning off the road. I just kept on going west. I know I didn't have any set plan in my head; I just wanted a lot of answers to a lot of questions. Why had he done the things he'd done to me and the girls? Did he still love me? Was he sorry for what he'd done to the family? Was he really my dad or not?

A good few miles down the road, when it dawned on me where I was heading, I phoned Tracey. 'I need to sort this thing,' I told her. 'I need to see him.'

'You're lying,' she said, 'aren't you? You're just going

out with your friends again to do more drugs, aren't you? I thought this was going to be a new start for us, Stuart, but you aren't going to change, are you?'

I switched the phone off and just kept driving west. I could understand exactly why she would think the way she did; I'd let her down often enough in the past, why should she have faith in me any more? But there wasn't enough space in my head to think through what I might be doing to our relationship, the best relationship I had ever had in my life. Feelings, thoughts, memories, confusion and enormous pain were all mixed together. The thing I wanted most of all was to try to make some sense of it all, to find some sort of resolution with the past.

Chapter Two

MUM AND THE BIN MAN

*H*e always seemed to be there, part of my life – my dad. But it must have been around 1972 that he first started courting Mum. He would be in the garden, sweeping up for her, or coming round to see us, bringing sweets, or presents that he'd picked up on his bin rounds. He was a great collector, was Dad, a real magpie. Anything he found that he thought still had any life in it he would cart home: furniture, broken toys, even a telly, which was the first we'd ever had. From having absolutely nothing, our house suddenly started to fill up with stuff that other people didn't want, much of which we needed badly and some of which just cluttered the place up.

His bin round was in an area of Ashton-under-Lyne where the residents threw out things that were better than anything we had ever had. Some of the things still worked. The telly did sometimes if you banged it very hard on the side in just the right place. Most of the time the screen was pierced with a single, tiny white dot.

I would get up close and try to peer through the dot, in the hope of seeing the picture through it, like a 'What the butler saw' peep show. My efforts were usually only rewarded by a short period of blindness while my eyes tried to refocus. I loved pushing the buttons in and out. I discovered that if I pressed two together they stuck in, but if I pressed a third button it would release them. Intrigued by these experiments I tried pushing all six while Mum was out at work, and they all jammed. Dad was furious, slapping me hard on the backs of my legs, making my skin burn, punching and kicking me until I went numb.

'Please, Daddy, no! I'm sorry!'

He threw me up the stairs and I dragged my battered body to bed, sobbing myself to sleep, crying for my mum. I was so sorry for being such a naughty little boy. I wanted to turn the clock back to just before I'd committed my crime and to make my daddy love me again. I vowed to myself that I would make an extra effort to be good for him.

He was always very scruffy, as you might expect a bin man to be, always wearing his welly boots however hot the weather, but no small boy worries about details like that. I was often out in the street with no clothes on at all myself, caked in dirt. None of the men round our estate was exactly what you would call smart, although Dad was probably one of the worst. He was big, over six feet tall with black hair, which he would wear with a side parting on the left. I would watch him combing it over with his left hand in the mirror and then patting the top of his head to flatten it out, imitating the action even though I had hardly any hair of my own. He had a moustache too, although it never seemed to grow that well. Thinking back now, I suppose that was because he was still a young man himself, barely out of his teens. When he was around the house he liked listening to sentimental songs like 'Seasons in the Sun' and 'Tie a Yellow Ribbon Round the Old Oak Tree', or anything by the Carpenters.

He had a slight limp from some childhood accident, and there was always a skirmish of dogs swirling around his boots. Mum had her Alsatian, Tina, and Dad had his Jack Russells, Bobby and Trixie – a working man's terriers, dogs that were quick enough to catch a rat when necessary and intelligently loyal to their master. Mum had got Tina while she was living on her own with us, as protection. This was a time when the Moors murders were still fresh in people's minds, when lone women felt nervous and vulnerable.

Our street was full of big families with no money. Most of them had no fathers around either, the mothers struggling to bring up as many as ten children on their own, in any way they could. Most of the kids would have different dads and even some of the women weren't sure who the fathers were. My sisters and I felt special because we had a dad and we believed he would protect us if we needed it, because he was big and tough and hard. I believed fervently he could fight anybody and win; he was the best, my dad; he was my hero.

Mum had been brought up in Mullingar, in Southern Ireland. My Nana came over to England to get work, promising to send for the children once she was settled. Mum loved it in Ireland, living with her Grandma Lacey. But when my Nana met and married a man called Albert in England she sent for her children and Mum had to leave Ireland.

After an unhappy few years, Mum met George Heywood. She was sixteen and he was much older, some-where around forty. She stumbled getting off a bus one day and had to go to hospital. The ambulance that arrived to take her was already carrying George, which was how they met. She always said she married him to get away from her family life, and I have no reason to doubt her. Their first baby, Shirley, was born in 1965 with spina bifida and other problems. Christina followed a year later, at a time when Shirley was being operated on in another part of the same hospital. I came along two years after that in 1968. Life for Mum at that stage must have seemed hopelessly tough, but she never considered giving any of us up or handing us over for someone else to look after.

There wasn't even enough money to buy me a cot, so I would sleep in drawers or whatever Mum could find to hold me. Then I was put into a bed with Christina, which I liked because it made me feel loved and comforted, although it meant that if one of us wet the bed both of us got wet. Sometimes we would share with Shirley as well but if we wriggled in the night we would catch her spine, making her cry out in pain.

George, I'm told, proved to be a heavy drinker and a bit of a womanizer, and found the strains of family life, particularly with a disabled child, too much to handle. He and Mum parted soon after I was born, although she was always vague about the exact timing, and the council moved us all to a semi-detached house in Smallshaw Lane on the Smallshaw estate. I guess our area was where they put troublesome families whom they thought might disturb the tranquillity of nicer neighbourhoods. There were no fences or gates; doors were always open, with people going neighbouring all the time, scrounging knobs of butter or cups of sugar off one another. There was always a whiff of hostility in the air as everyone struggled to ensure their own survival.

Knowing that I was too young to remember any different, Mum decided to pretend that George was nothing to do with me.

'You know,' she would say to me from time to time, when Dad wasn't around, 'you are a very special little boy. You know you really are your Dad's, don't you? He's not the real father of the girls, but he is yours. But we don't want to make the girls feel left out, do we? So we'll pretend he's your stepdad too.'

I felt sorry for the girls, having a different dad who had gone off and left them, but proud that Dad was mine, even if he did have his faults. Knowing who my dad was meant I knew who I was and where I'd come from. He gave me an identity that not many of the kids around our way could hope for. What kid doesn't want to have a real dad? Sometimes Mum would spot George in the street and point him out to the girls, and I felt I was better than them because my dad was the one taking care of us at home while George had deserted them. In my mind my dad was better than theirs.

'You're my fucking son,' Dad would say to me sometimes, almost as if he was angry with me for allowing any element of doubt in the matter.

There were no carpets on the floor in our house, nor in most of the houses in Smallshaw, and no curtains at the windows. Families that wanted privacy would stick up newspapers, or smear Windolene on the panes, which would serve the dual purpose of keeping out prying eyes and providing us with a canvas to play noughts and crosses or draw silly faces on. My earliest memory is of sitting outside the front of the house in the dirt, digging a hole with a discarded lollipop stick.

Things just kept coming through the door as Dad increased his collection. There was a PVC suite to replace our ripped and stained old sofa. The arrival of new furniture would always bring a troop of neighbours in to have a look, to admire or to mutter jealously.

'This will be good for Shirley,' Dad announced. 'It won't soak up her piss and we can just wipe it.'

My sister Shirley was incontinent and the house always stank of urine, although it wasn't all hers. The smell of urine, dogs and fags pervaded everything. The grown-ups were always having to change poor Shirley because there was nothing she could do about it herself. The trouble with the plastic material on the new suite was that it stuck to the backs of our bare legs after we had been sat on it for a while, and it would hurt to tear ourselves away, like ripping plasters off cuts.

I never realized when I was tiny that we were washed less often than most kids, that we were always dirty and covered in dog hairs. It was only when other kids started to take the mickey that the penny dropped. We always wore shorts, swapped between me and Christina, and Mum would only ever buy us new stuff from jumble sales, or nick it off the washing lines of the better-off areas.

We were always being sent out to scrounge things off the neighbours. Once I'd been given whatever I'd been sent to ask for I would walk back home slowly. If it were margarine it would be wrapped in a bit of foil and would start to melt, giving me a chance to lick the sweetness from my dirty hands. Mostly we ate jam and sugar butties, or sometimes lard or dripping. Anything we could get hold of we crammed into our mouths to stave off the continuous pangs of hunger.

The ice cream man hated coming up our street because he always got hassled for broken lollies and wafers; twenty kids all milling round the van shouting at him at once. Sometimes he would feel sorry for me if he found me on my own and would give me a chocolate flake. 'Don't tell the others,' he'd warn, and I never did.

Mum always seemed to owe people money and we would have to hide behind the sofa if men came knocking at the door. Because I was the youngest in the family and most innocent looking, she would send me to the chip shop most days, usually with no money. 'Tell them you've forgotten it,' she would say.

I hated doing it, but I hated being hungry even more. When the lady behind the counter asked for the money I would burst into tears. She would then feel embarrassed in front of the other customers and tell me to bring it later. After a while she started asking for the money before she served me. In those days you could take your own plate to the chip shop to be filled up. Mum would send me with a bowl, which the lady would fill up with gravy, giving us more to go round. Even when I was only two or three years old I would lurk outside the chip shop late in the evening asking customers for a chip as they came out with their dinners, having spent the evening in the pub. If they were in a really good mood they would buy me a whole portion of my own.

Shirley's spina bifida meant she had a hole in the middle of her back and this caused a deformity of the spine. She was paralysed from the waist down and didn't have any control or any mobility or any feeling in her legs. She was also hydrocephalous, a condition creating fluid around the brain. There was nothing wrong with her mind, but she had to be constantly lifted and cared for and had a shunt to drain the excess fluid from around her brain. She had a hump on her back as well, which was the result of an operation to stitch over the hole in her spine. Life had been cruel to her from the moment she was born.

To make matters worse, she also had epileptic fits from time to time. She always knew when they were coming because her mouth would get dry and she would start smacking her lips together. The first time I saw it happen I was about five years old. Mum and Dad had gone out for the night, leaving us on our own. It didn't bother us. As a small kid Shirley was always in and out of hospital with Mum, which meant Christina and I were often left to fend for ourselves.

'I don't feel well,' Shirley told us that evening. 'I think I might be about to have a fit.'

The next thing she was shaking in her wheelchair and there was white foam coming out of her mouth. I remembered Mum saying we had to get her tongue out so she didn't swallow it, but we didn't really understand what that meant. Christina ran to the kitchen and came back with a big dessert spoon and I tried to prise her teeth open with it, screaming and crying: 'She's dying, she's dying!'

Eventually I couldn't stand it any longer and ran to get my aunt from a few doors away, who came and laid Shirley out in the recovery position on the floor.

Christina and I loved Shirley and felt sorry for her; there were so many things you couldn't do in a wheelchair at the beginning of the Seventies. All the local cinemas and theatres, and a lot of the shops, had steep steps and no access for wheelchairs. We were always trying to find things to do that would cheer her up. One day, when Mum was outside hanging up the washing, we were sitting on Shirley's bed. I had found a box of Swan Vesta matches and had beckoned Christina to come to Shirley's room with me. Perching on the bed beside her I started to strike them, one by one, letting her blow each one out like a candle on a birthday cake, which made her laugh. Match after match flared and was snuffed. It felt good to be able to make her happy.

'Let me do one,' Christina demanded.

'No.' I turned away. 'I'm doing it. I found them.'

Christina made a lunge for the matches so I stretched my arms out at full length to keep them away from her and struck another.

Christina grabbed my arm and shook it. The match fell and the nylon bedclothes seemed to ignite instantly, the flames leaping to the curtains and spreading within seconds. Christina and I jumped up, screaming for Mum, wanting to run away, but Shirley couldn't move, and the flames were spreading over her lifeless, motionless legs as we desperately tried to wave them away. Mum ran in and ripped away the curtains and sheets, smothering the flames. But it was too late; Shirley's legs had ballooned up, red and blistered, and then blackened like charcoal. She couldn't feel any pain, but she could smell the charred flesh just as we could. Mum picked her up, cradling her in her arms, shouting furiously at us, and we watched in horror and bewilderment as she carried

Shirley out of the smoke-blackened room. We were sure we'd killed her, and although she survived she was horribly burned and had scars that never really healed.

Having a dad who brought home stuff made us better than everyone else in the street, that's how I saw it. All the others used to come round our house to watch the telly, when it was working, sometimes as many as twenty people at a time all crammed into our front room, with Mum at the centre of it all. We didn't own a kettle so there were always people in the kitchen boiling up pans of water to make themselves hot drinks. Mum was only in her early twenties and liked having friends around her. She always loved a party. We would often wake up and find that other people were sharing our beds, having crashed out after too much drink, empty cans and bottles everywhere. The thing Christina and I hated the most was the way the grown-ups all smoked so much. We used to get up early while they were all still unconscious and go round the house collecting up all the packets of cigarettes we could find and then hiding or destroying them.

One day Dad brought home a washing machine, and from then on all the neighbours would bring their washing round for Mum to do. There were always bags of dirty clothes everywhere, adding to the chaos and the smell.

There was always a lot of thieving going on around Smallshaw because it was the only way some families could survive. The women would bring back the stuff they had lifted from the shops, whether it was margarine or tins of coffee, and would share it all out. It sounds like everyone was getting on with one another when I put it like that, but there was always a current of jealousy and resentment bubbling below the surface, waiting for an excuse to surface.

'It's all right for Maureen,' the other women would mutter to one another behind Mum's back, 'with all her things.'

Dad even had a van and used to take us out on drives, which made the other families even more resentful. We came back one day to find the house had been broken into and robbed. Everyone knew it had been people from the street but there was nothing we could do about it and Mum said she wanted to move to a better area. Our gas and electricity meters were always being broken into for coins, food was stolen from our cupboards, and nothing was ever safe. The Electricity Board sent some men round to cut us off, but when they saw Shirley in her wheelchair they refused to do it.

Mum was often down the road at work in the off-licence and we would be left in the care of older children, who would bully us and drag us about the place, and beat me with sticks. It was just the way life was for us.

'You want to come round to our house for ice cream?' the older boys would ask me. I always said 'yes' because I was always hungry, and I always fell for it when they force-fed me a spoonful of margarine. I so much wanted the offer to be genuine I was always willing to give them the benefit of the doubt one more time.

There were some swings in a nearby park and we used to play a game where we jumped off in mid-air. I would always fall and graze my legs, which would mean Mum would stick me in the sink when I got home, using a scrubbing brush to try to get the tiny stones out of the cuts. I would fight and wail.

'Keep still,' she'd grumble, 'or you'll have to go to hospital for an operation.'

There was no way I wanted to risk that. I'd seen how Shirley would disappear to the hospital for days on end and then come home covered in bandages. When I did eventually have to go to hospital, because of measles, I was amazed to find it was actually more like a magical kingdom than the chamber of horrors I'd imagined. I was pampered by the nurses and given proper food three times a day for the first time in my life. The whole place felt warm and loving and there was nothing to fear, everyone smiling and laughing all the time despite the fact that we were all sick or in pain. I saw our home life in a different light after that, realizing for the first time that not everyone in the world was always angry and shouting at their kids.

We were always having to be treated for nits as well. Christina and Shirley both had Mum's thick ginger hair, which made the nit comb much more painful for them than for me. As they struggled and squawked she would tell them how blessed they were to have such long, thick hair. I was more of a strawberry-blond colour and had my head shaved most of the time.

There were some new houses being built down the bottom of Smallshaw Lane, which meant there were wagons full of earth streaming up and down all day long. A bunch of us used to stand at the top of the road and shout out to the men driving the trucks to give us rides. For a while they obliged and then the foreman told them to stop. The other kids persuaded me to hide in the bushes and jump out in front of one of the huge vehicles at the last moment, forcing the driver to stop with an explosive hiss of air brakes.

'What you fuckin' playing at?' he wanted to know.

'I don't know where my mummy is,' I replied, as I had been instructed, and started crying.

'Come on up here then,' he said, his heart softening.

As soon as he opened the cab door the others would all troop out of the bushes.

'Fuckin' ell, your mammy's been busy.'

The ruse worked every time, and usually resulted in us getting to share their lunch and drinks. Once they dropped us off on the site we would play happily amongst the diggers and tractors.

Quite often it was just me and Christina in the house because Shirley would be in hospital having operations on her legs, head and back, or my Nan would be looking after her. She and my Granddad Albert lived about five miles away and we often used to go over as a family for Sunday lunch. Granddad was a short, sturdy sort of chap who used to shout at me a lot. They lived in a private house and had lots of ornaments everywhere, like an

Aladdin's cave, which I just ached to pick up and look at but wasn't allowed to. They had a little dog, Sparky, who felt so soft and smelled so clean compared to our filthy, smelly dogs. On the way home after Sunday lunches Christina, Shirley and I would lie on the floor of the van, half asleep, and I would watch the orange streets lights flashing past the windows and imagine we were on a magic carpet ride.

Sundays were good because we could go to Sunday school, which the Salvation Army organized in a hut a few doors down from our house. We would sing songs and be told stories and even did some colouring-in of pictures of Jesus. They would give us presents like little gollywogs holding banjos and other musical instruments. They were the sort of thing you could have got for free off jam jars, but we loved them because they were pretty much the only presents we were ever given.

Chapter Three

THE PEN

Dad had an allotment. Not one of those little strips of vegetables with a makeshift shed at the end, but about an acre of land, like a smallholding, filled with ramshackle outbuildings. It was known as 'the pen'. Sometimes there would be twenty or thirty kids following him across the wooded piece of land behind the house and up the hill to the pen, with Shirley in her wheelchair, making him look like some sort of grubby Pied Piper.

The ground amongst the trees along the route was always strewn with litter and the pen itself was surrounded by a makeshift wall of house doors, so that no one could break in and passers-by couldn't see what was going on. It was Dad's little private kingdom. Behind the wall and padlocked gates was another world where he raised chickens, geese, ducks and pigs and stored yet more scrap salvaged from his rounds. There was a big black boar called Bobby, and a sow, terrifying, stinking great creatures that wallowed and snuffled in their own filth. An abandoned car stood, stripped and rusting, just inside the gates, waiting for someone to turn it into scrap.

In one of the sheds lived my dad's dad, whom we knew as 'Granddad from the Pen', a dirty, toothless old man who would always smell of whisky and grab me between my legs, or pinch my bum and rub his bristly chin against my face, which he thought was funny but which hurt. His clothes, which he wore day and night, were rags, like a tramp would wear. He also thought it was funny to throw his false teeth at me, even though I hated it. Dad used to do the same thing sometimes with his. Even at that age I could sense there was something about Granddad from the Pen that wasn't trustworthy.

I think his wife must have chucked him out years before and he went to live with Auntie June, Dad's sister, but she got fed up with him too and now he just had a camp bed in the corner of one of the sheds. He kept a pile of dirty books underneath the bed, which he was happy to get out for us, making us giggle with embarrassment and exclaim in horror. I'm sure the magazines must have been rescued from the dustbins, just like everything else in our lives. Granddad from the Pen spent a lot of his time down the pub. Only later did I discover he was an alcoholic; then I just knew he always smelt of booze, like Dad, only worse.

There had been some sort of falling out between Mum and Granddad from the Pen, although I never knew the details, but he stayed away from the house for a while. The day he did come back he came with a present for me, a pink bike. I didn't care what colour it was, it was a bike, something that none of the other kids in Smallshaw had, unless they were old ones with solid tyres that you couldn't use to jump on and off kerbs without jarring every bone in your body. Granddad from the Pen was obviously drunk, having just come out of the pub, and went in to see Mum, leaving me outside with my new possession.

I set off proudly to pedal round the neighbourhood. It was a glorious summer's day and I felt like the king of the area, until I was stopped by a policeman, who enquired where I'd got my bike from.

'It's a present from my Granddad,' I said, wondering why the policeman was being so nasty.

'I think we should go and talk to your Granddad,' he said. It turned out Granddad had nicked the bike off some little girl when she got off to go into her house just as he was passing. It broke my heart to see the policeman taking it away.

Going up to the pen was like visiting a little zoo, and all the local kids loved it. We would play hide and seek and other games. They would always be coming round pestering to find out if we were going up there. I used to love to root through the drawers around the sheds because they were always crammed with so much rubbish, just like our house. It seemed like a treasure trove to a four-year-old, another Aladdin's cave, although a bit different to my Nana and Granddad Albert's.

The pen was one of four, like some peasant farms left over from the Middle Ages, partially illuminated at night by the street lamps on the lane outside. It wasn't far to walk, but it was hard for me to keep up with Dad's long legs when it was just him and me going up there. If it was just us he would grow impatient with waiting for me to catch up and would stride off ahead, forcing my little legs to go faster, almost as if he didn't want anything to do with me, as if he was trying to get away. If Mum was with us he would put me on his shoulders, but if it was just us he would become angry as I lagged behind and would grab my hand and drag me off my feet, nearly jerking my arm out of its socket. Dad would go up to the pen every day because the animals needed feeding. He would collect any bit of food he could get his hands on and boil it up in big pans at home, adding the scent of pigswill to the existing smells of pee, dogs and fags.

The pen was a great place for a small boy to go, but sometimes I would make Dad cross and there would be flashes of nastiness as he gave me a push or a pinch to let me know I had disappointed him yet again. I knew that I must always be good and never anger him. He was only in his early twenties at that time, but he had a presence even then that made me wary. I had a feeling that he didn't like me and I was willing to do anything in order to change that. He used to insist that I collected the eggs from under the hens, which used to terrify me. They made so much fuss, flapping their wings and pecking at me with vicious beaks. I never wanted to do it, but I knew I had to do what he told me because he was my dad and he wasn't someone you would disobey. He used to keep ferrets as well, to help keep down the rat population, and he liked to put them down his trousers, and down mine. It was a horrible experience, feeling their claws digging in, believing they were biting, but he thought it was funny and that I should learn how to be brave about it. He was always trying to 'make a man' or 'make a farmer' of me.

I didn't like the way he would read magazines full of women while he was having a wee; at least I thought that was what he was doing. It was a bit confusing and very frightening.

Violence and bullying were the norm around Smallshaw. There was one family in particular who used to bully everyone. We used to go round to their house quite a bit, even though we thought they were disgusting, often ending up sleeping on their couches or several of us to a bed. Their mother was a big brute of a woman with no teeth, who used to sit there with her legs apart and no knickers on. Even as kids, Christina and I knew she was repellent. She would get her boys to give her love bites on her neck so people would think she had a man. She organized all the robbing in the area, like a sort of modern Fagin, sending the kids off to pinch clothes off washing lines, taking the spoils back to her house to be shared out. She was always picking fights and her kids followed her example.

One day Christina got into a fight with one of her daughters in the street and came in crying. I think she'd had clumps of her bright red hair pulled out in the heat of the battle. That family was always fighting and bullying one another and anyone else they could pick on, but this time Mum decided it had gone too far and went round to tell their mum what she thought of her. Christina and I watched from the window as the two women set to fighting in the street outside, punching and scratching and kicking, until eventually Mum came back in with blood all over her face. I was frightened but proud at the same time that our Mum wasn't scared to stand up to such a woman. She had stood up for Christina, just like I liked to believe Dad would have stood up for me in the same circumstances.

'It's all right, Mum,' I kept saying, trying to calm her crying when she came back in, cuddling her and wiping away the blood.

That fight was the final straw that convinced Mum and Dad that we should move from the street. Just at that time Dad's sister, June, announced she was moving out of her house in Cranbrook Street, a much better area, and asked Dad if he would like to buy it off her. Moving to the 'private sector' was like moving to another world for us. I guess Dad must have been able to get a mortgage at a good rate, working for the council, because they started to lay plans.

Despite this good news, there had been another incident that had left me troubled. We were on a family holiday to North Wales. We had driven down there in Dad's old Transit van, which was always getting punctures and having to pull over for repairs, but we would all be piled happily into it, with me, Christina and Shirley sitting or lying on mattresses in the back. Travelling loose like that was hard for Shirley because she was always in so much pain and there was nothing to stop her from bouncing and rolling about on every bump and corner. Christina and I would try to comfort her, reassuring her it would be all right, but the pain was terrible for her.

Dad's other sister, Doris, lived in a place called Penmaemawr, not far from Llandudno, and we stayed in a caravan at the Robin Hood camp in Prestatyn. I had never stayed in a caravan before and it all seemed like a great adventure. Being able to go to the seaside was so exciting and it reinforced the feeling we had that we were special and better than the other families around us in Smallshaw Lane. No one around our way ever went on holiday and I felt proud to have a dad who could organize such a treat.

Still being so small, just four years old, the beach appeared enormous. We spent the first afternoon building sandcastles and the girls were as happy as I was to be playing somewhere where there was no one picking on us or trying to spoil our fun. We felt completely carefree. At some point I decided to go down to the water by myself. The tide was out and I had to splash for what seemed like miles across the wet sand to get to the sea. The sky was bright blue above my head and the ocean stretched away forever into the distance, its edges lapping and rolling across my bare feet as I danced with delight in the foam, the rest of the world forgotten, including my family sitting behind me on the beach.

Back on the dry sand Mum must have noticed that I had strayed too far for safety, and Dad must have told her not to worry, that he would go and get me. I didn't hear him coming, didn't hear him calling me to come back, then suddenly I was aware of his presence and he was on me, grabbing me hard, hurting me.

'You naughty little bastard,' he yelled as he squeezed me with all his might. 'I've been shouting for ages.'

'I'm sorry, Dad, I didn't hear you. I was splashing.'

'You are a fucking liar. You're just plain fucking naughty, aren't you?'

He punched me to the ground, forcing my face down in the sand so that it filled my mouth and nose and eyes.

'Do you want me to tell your mum that you have spoilt the fucking holiday and you've ruined it for your sisters? Do you? Do you?' Every question was punctuated by another punch.

'No, Daddy, please.' I tried to speak through mouthfuls of sand. 'I'm sorry.'

I was struggling in his powerful grip, unable to breathe, panicked. After what seemed like forever he yanked me up.

'Get up, you little cunt, and stop fucking crying. If you don't stop crying I'll tell Mum you've been bad and naughty.'

As he let go of me I pulled myself up on wobbly legs, still able to feel his grip on my neck. Dad was cross with me and I just wanted to please him, and I didn't want him to tell Mum how naughty I was.

'Now get back there and put a smile on yer fucking face.'

My legs were shaking as I tried to run to obey him, shocked and unable to understand what I'd done wrong. I just knew that I must try much harder to be good, so he wouldn't be angry with me, so he would love me. I tried to hold his hand as we made our way back to Mum and the girls but he pulled it away and walked too quickly for me to keep up as I stumbled along.

'Have you been having a good time?' Mum asked when we reached her, and I just smiled and nodded, not able to trust my voice to be steady.

Starting school, just a little way from our house, was an eye-opener, like my visit to hospital. The teachers were so kind and caring, so different from the adults in my home world. The kids in the class were different from the ones who played in our street and came round our house. They didn't want to pull my ears or my hair or hit me or be nasty to me. When I realized what a friendly world it was it was like a huge weight lifting off my shoulders.

There were crayons and pens and paints, drums and even a violin, which I'd never seen before, and I was allowed to touch them and use them and everyone encouraged me and praised whatever I did. No one seemed to think I was naughty. There were some familiar faces from our estate, which was comforting once I realized they were going to behave differently at school from the way they behaved in the streets and houses. It was such a relief to be somewhere that didn't seem at all threatening or frightening.

Shirley had to go to a special school because of all her physical problems, so she would be picked up in a taxi or ambulance each morning, and Christina and I would make our own way to and from our school. One afternoon we came home to be told that we were going to be moving to Auntie June's house in Cranbrook Street. From now on, Mum explained, it would be our house. Overcome with excitement, I begged for us to go round and look at it, and Dad agreed to take me and Christina round there.

It wasn't far, so we walked there together, him striding ahead in his Wellingtons, us galloping along, trying to keep up as he cut down all the back ginnels and alleys. We'd been there before, to visit our cousins, who seemed spoiled to us, always having everything that we didn't – carpets, wall lights, proper cupboards in the front room, a gas fire in a stone-built fireplace and fancy patterned wallpaper. The carpet was purple and seemed to blend with the walls. I would get into trouble for keeping on turning the lights on and off because I'd never seen anything like it before. They even had a proper television, which worked all the time and didn't have to be hit. It seemed such a big, grand place, three storeys tall, and with its own cellar. We always wanted to stay there. Then it had been their house, but now it was ours and we could hardly contain ourselves.

As we approached the house that our dad was going to get for us, I looked up in awe. It stood at the centre of the terrace, its front door opening directly on to the street; the slot for the post low in the bottom of the glass front door – I hadn't noticed that before. I never knew you could have a letterbox there. It seemed like another sign that we were moving up in the world. The roof rose up to pointed eves, like the sort of houses families lived in on television. As Dad let us in it felt like we were walking into a big private castle.

The other kids in Smallshaw didn't let us get away without some teasing: 'Think you're better than us, do you, just because you're moving to a private house?'

'No, we don't,' we protested, but we did.

Christina and I ran from room to room, exploring every nook and cranny as we went. The attic rooms at the top of the house were going to be ours, which we thought were the best rooms in the house. It all seemed so huge, and in our rooms there were even wardrobes built into the eves that we could actually walk in and out of. I stood at the window, staring down, thinking it was thousands of miles to the pavements below, feeling a delicious little frisson of fear when I got too close to the sill. I felt like the king of the castle. Dad told us the council might give us a grant so we could build a special bedroom for Shirley, maybe even installing a lift so Mum didn't have to carry her up and down stairs all the time.

I did feel a little sad to be leaving some of the kids in Smallshaw who had been my friends, but I was too excited about moving away from the bullies to somewhere so new and different to grieve for long.

Chapter Four

A MORE PRIVATE WORLD

*T*he house in Cranbrook Street that had seemed like paradise on that first visit became as much of a junk heap as our house in Smallshaw within a few weeks of us moving in, filled with Dad's scroungings. He found a huge reproduction of Constable's famous *Hay Wain* picture on the bins and hung it in pride of place in the front room. I've never been able to see that picture since without thinking of him.

The house needed rewiring, but he didn't bother, so the electric heaters never worked. The power kept failing upstairs and we would have to run cables up the staircase in order to use any appliances or lights.

We moved to a new school and whereas we had fitted in with other kids from the streets of Smallshaw, most of whom were pretty much as dirty and scruffy as us, now I really stuck out. We tried to make some new friends, but I think we were seen as little more than street urchins by the neighbours. I got a bit of bullying and teasing at school for my appearance and because we obviously lived in poverty. Because I was getting used to Dad hitting me, every time I saw someone raise their hand I would immediately fall to the floor and roll into a ball, covering my head to protect myself from the blows I knew were coming. It wasn't long before the other kids realized how easy it was to get me to do this.

There wasn't the same culture of neighbouring as there had been in Smallshaw; people didn't just pop in and out of one another's houses and sit around for hours. We were left pretty much to ourselves and Dad started to become more and more of a tyrant in his own little kingdom. He started shouting at Mum a lot, especially after he had been to the pub. She could never do anything right. Cranbrook Street was perfect for him, with the pub on one corner and the chip shop on the other, and he soon developed a regular routine. He would be up on his bin round early and then into the pub between twelve and three, before coming home for a sleep.

He always smelled of the bins and once he'd pulled off his sweaty wellies he would sit with his feet in a bowl or pan of hot water, ordering me to wash them and scratch them for him. It was a disgusting job because they stank so badly. I would peel his socks off for him and they would be stuck to his feet, rock hard with sweat after spending so long in his boots.

As he got used to having control, he started to become stricter about the way our lives were run. Finding he had so much power went to his head. We started to be given definite bedtimes, when before we had pretty much run wild. He didn't like it if he had to carry Shirley around and if she wet herself he would shout at Mum to 'get her fucking changed'. The atmosphere was getting much worse, but he was still my dad and I still loved him. I had no one else to compare him with anyway.

After his afternoon nap he would wake up again about seven in the evening and go back down the pub. We would all try to get to bed before he reeled back in and the rows really started. We could hear the shouting and screaming downstairs and even then I knew Mum was getting beaten. He told her she had to get a full-time job to help with the money, and she did as she was told. Until then she had at least been there sometimes, or at least not far away, and suddenly she was gone for long periods of the day, and I felt lonely.

The glimpses of nastiness and aggression that I had seen up at the pen, which had exploded on the beach in Wales, now became regular occurrences, and they escalated almost daily.

'Don't touch those fucking crusts,' he would yell if I went to eat some bread. 'They're mine.' Whenever any of us had bread we had to cut off the crusts and give them to him if we didn't want a beating.

If I touched something that was his, or was naughty in any way, I would get battered. The trouble was I didn't always know when something I was doing would turn out to be on the forbidden list, although in the end it covered just about everything I did.

'Don't pick your nose!'

'Stop picking your nails!'

'Stop itching your bum!'

'Stop scratching your head! Have you got nits?'

'Dirty legs!'

'Dirty knees!'

'You're a filthy little bastard. Go and wash!'

'Look at the mess you've left round this basin and taps!'

'Clean the fucking soap.'

'Your bedroom's a mess.'

'You've left dirt on the sofa.'

'Your coat's dirty.'

'Your trainers are dirty.'

He had started grabbing me regularly, screwing my face up in his powerful fingers and slapping me round the head. He would suddenly appear behind me when I was least expecting it and slap me or throw me against the wall, knocking the breath out of my body. I wished I wasn't so naughty because it seemed my behaviour was making him really hate me, but I just didn't seem to be able to work out what I was about to do wrong next.

I was constantly scratching and itching because I always had nits and worms; it was impossible to stop myself, and it seemed to drive him mad. Sometimes I'd itch my bottom and pull out a whole handful of worms.

To deal with the nits, he decided I had to have my head shaved regularly, for hygiene, which revealed the little points I had on my ears, giving him the opportunity to tease me, calling me 'Spocky' after Mr Spock in *Star Trek*, or Kojak. The other kids at school were taking the piss too, warming their hands on the top of my head in the cold weather. I hated it all.

The more he went on at me, the more I just kept thinking, 'Please, Daddy, no,' but he never stopped, never let up on me. He was changing, becoming angrier every day, and more and more disgusted by me. I knew I must be bad and naughty, because he kept telling me I was. I knew I was ugly, because he kept telling me, so I could understand why it must be so hard for my parents to love me, but I didn't know what to do to make myself better and more lovable.

Sometimes I did know I was being naughty, and just wasn't able to resist temptation. We were nearly always hungry and he would eat chocolate biscuits in front of us and forbid us from having any; then he would go out, leaving the packet in full sight. Like most small boys I was unable to resist sneaking one, not realizing he had marked the packet before he went, and would receive a battering when he came back.

'Your dad's going to adopt the girls now,' Mum told me soon after we moved into Cranbrook Street, 'so we can be a proper family. Even though you really are his son, Stuart, we're going to play a game. We're going to go to the courts and pretend that he's adopting all three of you together, so the girls don't feel upset.'

I was willing to go along with that; it was a game we had been playing at home for as long as I could remember.

When we got to court, playing the charade of a happy family, wearing the first brand-new clothes I think I'd ever had bought for me, we were sat in front of two men and a woman. They asked a few questions.

'So, Stuart,' the lady said, 'do you like your new daddy?'

'I like my daddy,' I replied politely, 'but I don't like it when he hits me and hurts me.'

I glanced over and saw the look of anger flickering across his face. I smiled quickly, as I always did when I was afraid, and everyone started laughing, seeing the little exchange as proof that my dad and me could laugh and joke together. The adoption was approved.

Our days fell into a regular routine. After I came back from school Mum would be at work and I would be sent out to play, even though he would insist that Christina and Shirley went to bed with him for an hour for a rest. Now and then I would be allowed to join them for the rest and on one occasion Shirley started playing with my private parts.

'Gerroff Shirley,' I said, indignantly.

'Stop fucking about, you two!' he barked. 'Go to sleep.'

'She keeps playing with my widget!' I protested.

Shirley was always there in the afternoons after being brought back from her special school, a constant scowling presence in the corner of the sitting room in her wheelchair, her arms folded and her face unhappy.

On the afternoons when I was sent out I knew that if I came back before I was allowed, which was seven o'clock,

I would be in for a battering, so I never did. Even if I needed to go to the toilet I would find somewhere outside rather than disobey him and go into the house. I was not allowed to use the front door, always coming in through the back garden, which was the one part of our home that was kept neat and tidy, bracing myself for the expected battering.

I seemed to be an outcast from every group of children in the area, so it was hard to find things to do to fill the hours until I was allowed back into the house. I didn't look like the others at my new school because I was so dirty, I didn't sound like them and I didn't dress like them. But I no longer fitted in with the kids from Smallshaw either, because they thought I believed myself better than them.

There was a disused railway line running not far from Cranbrook Street and some of the older kids would make dens in the arches along the side, where they would meet to smoke and drink and sniff glue. If I couldn't find anyone else to play with I would wander up there on my own, finding some comfort in the wind that always seemed to whip along between the embankments. I was only five years old and the bigger boys would watch me from their dens, taking the mickey but not in a threatening way. They all had plastic bags and I would watch as they put them over their faces from time to time and breathed deeply of whatever was inside. They seemed quite friendly and I hung around on the edge, partly curious, partly desperate for company.

As I grew braver I would go into the dens with them when they invited me, pick up the bags and breathe deeply, as I had seen them doing. The fumes from the glue bottles inside the bags would make my ears buzz in a pleasant way, and my unhappiness and pain seemed to become fuzzy around the edges. I got a feeling of love and peace and nothing seemed to matter quite as much. By the time I got home I was walking in a semi-dream. When I got inside and Dad hit me it didn't hurt so much because I was already partly numb, and the glue would help me to fall asleep after my beating.

Once I had discovered it I liked the feeling and I would go back to the railway lines almost every day for the next five or six years. The bigger boys became used to having me around and were happy to share their escape route with me because they thought I was funny, like a live toy, a sort of mascot I guess. They all knew who I was and what my family was like. We were easily recognizable because of Shirley being in her wheelchair whenever we were out. Sometimes I would bring the glue home with me and take it up to my bedroom, so I could keep the feeling going later, when I needed it.

I always knew when Dad was angry with me because his upper lip would curl up at the sides, and the night that things got worse he was waiting for me inside the back door with that familiar look on his face.

'What fucking time do you call this?' he snarled.

I couldn't properly tell the time by then, but I had taught myself to recognize seven o'clock and I could see the hands were in the right place on the kitchen clock behind him. I tried to tell him that I wasn't naughty, that I had got it right, but he didn't seem able to listen to any reason and started to lay into me with a ferocity I had never experienced before, kicking and punching me so hard I was thrown around the room as if I weighed nothing and as if he didn't care how damaged I might become. Whenever I was terrified, which by then was most of the time, I used to experience a sort of buzzing noise all around me, like a static charge. It would get inside my head as well, as if all the sounds around me were slightly distorted. The fear constricted my throat, making it hard to talk or swallow. My chest would always hurt from sobbing.

'Get upstairs and get cleaned up, you little bastard,' he shouted, kicking and pushing me towards the stairs. 'And get to bed.'

I struggled to obey, my body feeling broken and painful. I was so cross with myself for being naughty again and making my father so angry. Why couldn't I just be a good boy? Why did I have to make him have to punish me? I had an overwhelming feeling of being so sorry as I sobbed into my pillow, wishing Mum would come home and give me a cuddle and tell me everything was all right. I tried to hug the wall, which was covered in footballing wallpaper, left over from when my aunt and uncle lived there. All I wanted was for my mum and my dad to love me, but I understood they couldn't for as long as I went on being such a bad little boy. I knew my mum wouldn't be able to cuddle me, because I'd heard Dad telling her not to. He said I needed to toughen up. Looking back now, I realize he was jealous of my relationship with her even then.

I don't know how long I lay there that night before he came upstairs to my room, pushing the door shut after him. I stayed as quiet as I could, determined not to do anything else to anger him. He lay down on the bed beside me and the familiar odour of his stale sweat enveloped me. He had never hugged me in his life, but he put his arm around me. I couldn't stop the tears from coming again.

'You know you're a naughty boy, don't you?' he said. 'You know I don't want to shout at you, but you have to learn.'

He started stroking me, which was comforting and strange. Then he took my hand and held it against himself, moving it rhythmically back and forth. The bed started shaking and after a few moments I could feel that he had peed on to my hand. He wasn't cross with me any more and I felt very happy to have been forgiven. It felt great to know that he thought I was a good boy.

'Are you hungry?' he asked.

I was always hungry.

'Wait up here,' he said, 'and I'll make you some potato hash. Come down in a bit.'

I lay there feeling happy with myself for the first time in a long while, wondering how long 'a bit' was, not wanting to spoil things by going down too soon or too late. I must have drifted off to sleep because he had to send Christina up to tell me the food was ready. I rushed down, expecting to be in trouble again, but he was still in a good mood when I got to the kitchen.

To have him pleased with me and to be given something to eat was wonderful. Even to this day I can't eat potato hash without remembering that first time. We used to eat it a lot, with meat that the butcher sold for pets, and vegetables, anything that was cheap. Nothing was ever thrown away or allowed to go to waste; everything was fried up again and again until every last scrap had been eaten. Sometimes I tasted the stuff he prepared for the pigs and it was nicer than the stuff we all ate.

Chapter Five

A VERY NAUGHTY BOY

*T*hat first time was the gentlest time, and although it was a little while before he became really violent, from then on the abuse in my bedroom became a regular feature of our daily family routine. The glow of approval after the first time didn't last long and his verbal abuse towards me escalated as quickly as the physical abuse.

'You're fucking ugly.'

'You're a bad boy and I'm getting the police to come and take you to a fucking home!'

'Your mum doesn't fucking love you.'

'I'm gonna give your mum a fucking beating, I'm really gonna hurt her, and it's because of you, because you're such a naughty little bastard.'

Every day was like a test, a horrible repeat of the day before but with some new insult or pain added on. He was becoming almost as bad towards Christina as well, even though I knew she wasn't naughty like me and worked really hard to try to keep the home going when

Mum was at work. He used to shout for us to come in when he was sitting down in the front room, and we would hurry to do his bidding. I was always smiling in the hope of defusing his anger, looking up at him, my head bowed, waiting docilely for whatever would come next. I was always nervous about looking at him directly. 'Are you eyeballing me?' he would demand if I looked up, and my eyes would shoot back to the floor.

'Fight each other,' he would order me and Christina. 'You both need to toughen up.'

There was no getting out of it, because if we didn't fight each other, really punching and kicking and slapping, then he would hit us, and he hit much harder than we did. Even if Mum was there, witnessing it, he didn't care.

'Stop it, David,' she would protest, but he overruled her, shouting encouragement at us like a trainer beside a boxing ring. All the time Shirley would just be sat there, in her wheelchair, watching the horrors going on around her, looking bored and bemused and sulky. If it was bad for Christina and me, God knows what it was like for her, day after day after day just sitting or lying around stinking of piss, listening to the shouting and watching the beatings.

After one of those fights he would send us up to bed, and I would be able to hear Christina sobbing in her room, just as I was in mine.

'Are you all right?' I would whisper, trying to send my voice across to her room but terrified he would be listening in and would exact some extra punishment.

'Yes,' she would gulp. 'Are you all right?'

'I'm so sorry.'

'I'm sorry too.'

We would keep on telling each other how sorry we were until one of us eventually fell asleep.

Whenever I came in the back door of an evening he would be lying in wait for me with some new complaint about my behaviour, and he would start shouting and punching and hurting me, spitting at me to show his contempt. It was all about power. I was never allowed to do anything without asking his permission.

'Dad, can I go to the toilet?'

'Dad, can I have a drink of water?'

'Dad, can I stand up?'

'Dad, can I sit down?'

I always assumed that he was right about everything, because he was a grown-up and he was my dad. If he said I was bad, then I must be. He watched my every single move, just waiting for me to put a foot wrong, constantly thinking up new rules that I mustn't break. If I sneaked myself a butty to eat and left a few crumbs, I would have to be punished in a frenzy of anger. If I had a slice of bread or a piece of cheese, or if I left a cup out, it didn't matter what I did, it was always wrong and meant I had to be taught a lesson, 'for my own good'. He took to checking my underpants and if I had left any sort of stain, which I often had if I had been to the toilet outside, I would have to be punished again. The questions he asked me made me squirm with embarrassment; no part of my life was private from his probing.

'Have you been shaking your willy after you've been for a wee?'

He would inspect me all over, checking my willy, then taking his own out to show me what it should look like. 'Feel it, so you know what it should feel like.'

He started stripping me naked in front of the girls and tying me up with ropes after beating me up at the back door, so tightly I couldn't get free however much I struggled or cried. Sometimes he would tie my hands and my neck to my feet so I would be twisted into painful shapes, as the dogs ran around me, barking with excitement at all the noise.

'Try and get out of that!' he would sneer as my panic mounted. 'Look at him, Shirl, look at him!'

Shirley would stare at me with blank eyes and an unchanging expression, knowing that if she said anything she ran the risk of him turning his wrath on to her.

My greatest priority was to be a good boy and make both my parents love me, so I never told anyone outside the family what was going on. I assumed it went on in lots of other houses as well and no one would be that interested anyway; they would just tell me not to be so naughty. And then there was the fear that if they found out how bad I was someone would tell the police and I would be taken away to a children's home. However bad my life with my dad might be, the unknown was even more frightening. At least in Cranbrook Street I had

Mum and my sisters. If I was taken to a home I wouldn't have anyone to love, nothing familiar to cling on to at the lowest moments.

Some days he would send me up to bed the moment I came in and then come up to batter me there, away from the girls. Then he would come up and lie next to me, telling me to masturbate him. I didn't like it, but at least it didn't hurt and I knew it would make things better – it was part of my punishment and afterwards he would be pleased with me. I would have done anything not to be battered any more.

There was an old sideboard in my room, which he'd brought back from his rounds but had been unable to sell, and sometimes I would open the cupboard doors and squeeze myself inside, holding my breath and hoping he wouldn't find me when he came up. But then I would become too scared of what would happen if he did catch me trying to hide from him and I would come back out and get into the bed to wait. Other times I would get into the walk-in cupboards that Christina and I had thought were such a game when we looked round the house. The place I felt safest was on the floor under the bunk bed, staring up at the slats, feeling like I was in a prison cell and couldn't be touched, but my nerve would always go before he actually came up to deal with me and I would crawl back out to face whatever was in store for me.

Given a choice between a battering and masturbating him, masturbating was always preferable. But after a few months it wasn't enough to satisfy him and he told me to put his penis in my mouth. Then he started masturbating himself over me, hurting me while he did it, pushing my face down so hard into the pillow that I had to struggle to get enough air, hitting and shouting abuse at me at the same time as relieving himself: 'You dirty little scum! You fucking maggot bastard!' The power he had over me with his great strong hands seemed to drive him to a frenzy of excitement.

Having started with checking my underpants he went on to inspecting my bottom whenever I came in, making me bend over so he could see if I was clean. I was always sore because of the worms and bad hygiene and he got some cream to treat the sore patches. He insisted on applying it, as if he were really a caring dad, but he actually played roughly with me with his fingers while he did it, which made me bleed when I went to the toilet. He started putting his erection between my legs and then moved on to pushing it inside my bottom, spitting into his hand to provide himself with the necessary lubrication. The sound of men hawking up phlegm still makes me shiver. The pain was immense and made me cry even though he wasn't being as vicious as before, as if he was trying to coax me into letting him do new things. Whenever I went to the toilet, once he had started penetrating me, there was usually blood in the bowl, which frightened me.

When he was doing things to me I would detach myself from what was going on, staring at the footballs on the wallpaper, just wanting it to be over as quickly as possible. I wished I wasn't such a bad boy all the time, so that I didn't always have to be punished.

After he had finished he would usually be quite nice to me for a while. He would sometimes put me in a warm bath and even to this day I still find it comforting to be immersed in warm water. Some nights he would take me with him in the van to pick Mum up from work at the bakery where she did her shifts. I used to like sitting between them on the engine cover on the way home because it was warm and it soothed my soreness through my pyjama bottoms. I would try to cuddle up as close to Mum as possible on the way back, without him seeing, just touching her arm or trying to smell her. It felt wonderful to have a bit of softness and kindness, even though I knew by then that she couldn't protect me from him.

There was a hatch in the floor under the stairs at Cranbrook Street, leading down to the cellar. Sometimes when I came in from playing and deserved to be punished Dad would beat me and strip me off and send me down the concrete stairs into the cold and damp room below instead of sending me up to my room. It was dank and there was always a puddle of stale water at the bottom of the stairs, which I had to paddle through in bare feet, trying to find a dry patch.

'You stay down there with the rats,' he would shout, before slamming the hatch shut, extinguishing the last sliver of light. I would feel round in the darkness with my bare feet, trying to find a dry patch to stand in. I would try to hug the walls for comfort but the damp made the plaster flake and it would come away to my touch, crumbling in my hands. It felt like even the wall was rejecting me and I would cry uncontrollably, realizing Dad must be right and I must be really, really naughty.

I had no way of knowing how long I was left down there, but it felt like hours. The chill would spread through my bones as I crouched there, hugging myself for warmth, teeth chattering and muscles trembling, waiting for the moment when he would decide I had learned my lesson and could be allowed back up into the light.

He started bringing things that he could use to hit me home with him from the rounds – a heavy buckled belt one day, a brass fork the next. He would keep these weapons beside him as he sat in his chair, lashing out at me with them whenever I displeased him, claiming he'd asked me to turn over the television or make him a drink and that I had ignored him. I knew it was all lies because I listened for every word, terrified of making a mistake. He didn't care how hard he hit, leaving bruises all over my legs.

He had his booty on display on the walls, everything from brass plates to ornamental swords with jewels in the handles, and nearly all of it could be used to inflict pain when he wanted it to.

'See this brass crocodile?' he'd say when he got home with some new trophy. 'It's for you.' And then he'd hit me with it.

The buckle on the belt used to cut my skin so deeply I would have to sit in a cold salt-water bath afterwards to bring down the marks he'd left. No matter how hard I fought to keep control the salt would sting and make me cry.

'See,' he'd say, standing over me as I shivered and sobbed in the cold water, 'this is what happens when you're a naughty lad. Why can't you be good?'

The teachers at school used to ask me where my bruises came from, but I didn't want them to know what a naughty little boy I was in case they sent me away to a special school. 'I've been out,' I would lie, 'playing army, climbing trees and that.'

It was easy for them to believe, I guess, because I used to fall over a lot at school, banging my head. Sometimes I even did it on purpose because I liked the attention it got me from the teachers when they put me on their knees and rocked me to comfort me and stop my tears.

Bath times were always frightening because I felt so vulnerable, being wet and naked. Sometimes he would come into the bathroom, tell me to open my mouth and then pee into it, thinking it was funny. Or he would grab hold of me, shove me under the water and hold me there.

I would thrash around in panic, trying to get back to the air, certain he was trying to kill me.

Often he would pee in the sink in the kitchen; sometimes he would do it while Christina was trying to wash up, doing it all over the pots and all over her hands. She used to make a huge effort to be cleaner and tidier than the rest of us, scrubbing her trainers and socks every night. She was mature for her age.

At other times he would make me eat some of the swill he had made for the pigs, or he would make me come downstairs in just my underpants.

'Sit there.' He would indicate the floor. Then he would feed the dogs next to me and ask if it smelt nice. I didn't know what to say because I knew he would hit me whatever I said. I would try to nod and shake my head at the same time, so it wasn't a yes or a no. Then he would rap his knuckles on top of my head over and over and say, 'You're a naughty little bastard. Nobody likes you.'

Sometimes I would just be sitting at the table and he would ram my face into my dinner with no warning. 'You're a naughty little bastard, aren't you?' he would say as I sat there with food all over my face.

'Yes, yes I am. Sorry, Daddy.'

If Christina had angered him he might punish us together, like the times when he would feed the dogs and then make us eat bread and milk out of the same bowls. 'This is what you would be eating if you were in prison,' he'd tell us. 'Make sure you eat it all up. Lick the bowl clean.'

He didn't seem to punish Shirley in the same way he punished us. I would see her crying sometimes and would wonder why, but I would never ask; we all knew better than to talk about personal things like that. Besides, I wouldn't have known how to start.

At night I used to make Christina tell me stories before I went to sleep. She had always been a bit of a reader when she could get hold of books, particularly at school. 'Tell me a story, Christina,' I would wheedle. 'Tell me about Goldilocks.'

If she didn't tell the story exactly the same way each time, forgetting some tiny detail, I would pick her up on it. If she tried to get out of her storytelling duties I would threaten to tell Mum and Dad that she'd been swearing, because she always was. 'I'll go downstairs and tell them,' I would threaten, although she must have known I would never have dared. She was always there for me, Christina, at home and at school, and I will always be grateful to her for that.

She was becoming like the mother of the house, especially when Mum was out at work, but she still cried a lot, like a little girl. She would try to cook my tea while I was out playing, heating up beans and stuff even though she couldn't really reach the stove properly. It always tasted pretty bad but I was happy to eat it; all the food in our house tasted bad so it made no difference. If you are hungry enough and you know there is nothing else coming, you'll eat whatever you're given. We used to pick chewing gum up off the streets and pop it into our mouths, chewing and spitting out the stones and dirt until it was clean and we could walk around feeling posh, like we were able to afford gum of our own.

The council gave us the money to build an extension in order for Shirley to have a room of her own with a lift, so she didn't have to share a bedroom with Mum and Dad, giving them more privacy as a couple. Shirley had had an operation and had a bag fitted so she didn't pee everywhere any more. The bag would fill up and we would have to empty it for her every few hours. We also had to try to keep her clean so she didn't get an infection where the tube went into her. It was an improvement to her life, but it hurt her sometimes because her skin would become sore where the bag was attached to her with stickers and we would have to clean her with surgical spirit and friar's balsam. The little stickers looked like silver smiles and Christina and I used to stick them over our mouths to make it look like we were smiling.

One afternoon I came in at the usual time, hot and tired from school and playing. Dad didn't attack me and seemed in quite a good mood for once, so I asked if there was any pop. He gave me a bottle of what looked like lemonade. Thirsty, I took a swig and immediately gagged, realizing he had tricked me with some of Shirley's urine. Not content with having executed his practical joke, he then forced me to keep drinking it. Seeing how much I hated it he added it to his list of regular tortures for me.

Chapter Six

OUR CLARE

When Mum discovered she was pregnant again, Dad told me that this time he was going to have a proper son, one who would be good. His words hurt, but I still looked forward to having a brother. The day Mum went into hospital, Dad came back home alone.

'Your mum died in childbirth,' he told us, collapsing down into a chair with his head in his hands.

The news was so terrible I could hardly take it in. How would we manage without her? If Mum were dead, we would be left totally at his mercy. Life would be unliveable without her. All three of us burst into tears of inconsolable grief and shock.

'I'm only kidding,' he said, apparently contemptuous of us for taking the joke so badly. 'She's had a girl. But it was a difficult birth; she could've died.'

We loved Clare to bits the moment Mum brought her home, even though she had some problems. She had borderline Down's syndrome, and hydrochephalus like

Shirley. For a while Dad acted differently, a bit more like a proud father, but as it became more obvious Clare had problems, his frustrations took hold again. He told Mum it was her fault that she had had two children with problems, that it showed she wasn't a fit mother. The doctors said it was just bad luck, as if our family needed any more of that, but he didn't believe them. He said Mum was useless because she couldn't even give him a son. I didn't understand why he would say that. She'd given him me, hadn't she? Was I really so naughty that I didn't even count as a proper son?

It was a relief to have Mum home from hospital, providing at least a bit of care and nurturing for us all, but at night we could hear her screaming downstairs and I knew that he was hurting her, just like he hurt me. None of us ever dared to go down to see what was happening. I didn't even dare to go to the bathroom in the night in case I came across Dad and he would be angry, so if I knew I couldn't hold on till morning I used to get up quietly and pee in a drawer or kneeling down on the carpet so it wouldn't make any noise and attract attention. No one noticed the smell because the whole house stank of urine anyway. Only years later did I discover that Christina was doing exactly the same in her room on the other side of the landing.

One night I did pluck up the courage to come out of my room for some reason in the middle of the night. I got as far as the top of the stairs and noticed that Shirley's door was open. Peering down through the banisters I saw that

Dad was lying on top of her and she was stretching out her hand, as if trying to reach me. I scurried back to my bed, not wanting to believe what I had seen. In the morning I told myself to forget the scene, convinced myself that I must have been mistaken. I had too much to think about already, I couldn't cope with any more.

Mum was as scared of him as we were, with all his shouting and violence. He would quite often throw his dinner at her for no good reason. She had given up work to have Clare but it wasn't long before he was telling her she had to get another job, and she went to work at the bakery on a shift from two till ten, leaving him alone with us again every afternoon and evening. Clare would cry a lot and Dad's answer was always to stuff some chocolate in her mouth. Her grown-up teeth turned black and had rotted away before they even had a chance to come through.

One night, when Clare was about six months old, she was crying so loud and so long I plucked up the courage to come out of my room again and tiptoed down to the next landing to see what was wrong, my heart thumping with fear at what I might find. I saw Dad bringing her out of their room, where her cot was, and I froze, terrified he would see me, unable even to run back to the safety of my room. As I watched he deliberately dropped her down the stairs. As she bounced from step to step, I wasn't able to stop my screams from escaping, making him look straight up at me. As she came to rest at the bottom, her screams echoing mine, Dad suddenly started acting as if it had been an accident. He ran down just as Christina came out of the sitting room and scooped up poor, crumpled baby Clare. All three of us were crying and Dad was insisting he had slipped and she'd fallen out of his arms. It was the first time for sure I knew he was lying about something. I'd seen exactly what he'd done. I couldn't understand it; she was only a baby, she couldn't have done anything naughty enough to deserve that, could she?

Left to his own devices for longer each day he became even nastier and I heard him shouting more and more at Christina and Shirley, which I knew wasn't fair. I could understand why he was always angry with me because I was such a naughty boy, but I knew the girls were never naughty, so I didn't think it was right for him to punish them. Christina spent her whole time trying to do things for us, and Shirley couldn't move far enough to do anything bad. They were complete innocents, so why was he so angry with them?

When Clare was three or four years old he used to tell me he was going to kill her while I was away at school. 'I'll burn her fingers in the fire,' he'd say, and laugh when I cried out at the thought. I had no doubt he was capable of doing such a thing, and each day during our morning break at school I would sneak out through some bent railings at the back of the playground, run all the way round the back of the houses, let myself into our back garden and creep towards the house, squeezing myself behind the shed, terrified he would look out of the window and see me. When I reached the house I would turn over the mop bucket, which always stood by the back door, and raise myself up just high enough to peer in through the downstairs window, holding my breath in case I gave myself away, desperate to see Clare moving around and to check he hadn't hurt her. Sometimes, if the windows were open, I would be able to hear him upstairs with Mum in the bedroom and the sounds would make me feel sick, but I would still hang on, my heart thumping with fear, until I had seen Clare and put my mind to rest enough to go back to school.

He would always draw the curtains when he was watching the television in the early evening, so we were cut off from the outside world completely. We would all be in the room together and he would fetch his filthy magazines out and get us to look at the pictures. Sometimes they were just women in poses, sometimes couples doing things, sometimes they were pictures of men and close-up shots of erect penises. I didn't want to look at any of them.

'Look at her,' he'd say to me, pointing to some pouting, naked girl. 'Do you think she's a virgin? Look at her fanny.'

'What do you think of that?' he'd ask Christina, showing her another picture. 'Look at the tits on that.' Then he would grab Shirley's breasts in front of us and laugh.

Sometimes he would show us dirty films on the wall with an old cinematic projector. We hated them but he wouldn't let us leave the room while they were on. He said we needed to learn what life was about. 'Please, Daddy, no,' we would plead. 'We don't want to watch these films.' He would take films of us as well, although we never knew what he did with them.

He would make us go upstairs and put on Mum's little shorty nighties, dressing us up like dolls and then just making us sit there in the lounge with him. (Much later, I found out that he used to enjoy wearing Mum's clothes himself sometimes, telling her he liked the feel of the material on his skin.) He had complete power over all of us, able to make us do whatever he wanted. We were all so traumatized we never found a way to talk to one another about the things that were happening and how we felt about them. All three of us just did as we were told, until he eventually left us alone and we could get on with our own lives together for a few hours.

He would put the chain on the front door whenever he was messing about with us, in case Mum came home early, which she did once or twice.

'Why's the chain on the door?' she wanted to know, when she finally managed to attract his attention and was let in.

'Because I was upstairs in the bathroom,' he said quickly, 'and I forgot to take it off again.'

Now that I was eight or nine years old, I would see other boys at school sometimes who had managed to get hold of dirty magazines like Dad's. They would huddle in corners giggling over the pictures and want me to look at them too, but I was terrified, thinking they were all going to turn out to be like him. Everything was so frightening and confusing. On my way home from the school yard each day I used to hug the wall and cry, trying to get some comfort out of the cold stones.

However often experience taught me that nothing good would ever happen in our family, I always remained hopeful, especially as Christmas approached and all the other kids at school started to talk about the presents they hoped they would get. One Christmas morning, even before I opened my eyes, I was aware Dad was in my room. He was leaning over the bed, staring at me. I smiled at him hopefully, feeling excited at the prospect of at least one day of love and attention.

'What are you fucking smiling at?' he wanted to know.

'Has Father Christmas been?'

'Yeah, he's been.' I followed the direction of his gaze to a potato lying on the bed. 'There you go.'

'What do you mean?'

'Eat it.'

He sat and watched as I took a bite and started to chew, trying to force my tensed throat to accept the bitter-tasting pulp and swallow.

Everything he ever gave us was rubbish. He once came home with a sack filled with old broken toys that someone had thrown out.

'There you are,' he said to me. 'I've got you a train set.'

He laughed at me as I took it up to my room and sorted it all out on the floor. It was exciting to have something constructive to do and I really wanted to get it working, to show him how clever I was. I went downstairs and found an old piece of Brillo and set about cleaning up the track, rubbing and polishing the years of grime away until it shone like new. All the time I was thinking, Fuck off, fuck off, fuck off. I was never allowed to swear out loud. It took hours of work, and I would get little electric shocks every time I touched it, but I actually managed to get the whole thing working, even the little light on the front of one of the trains. I used to put the light on at night, when the house was shrouded in gloom, and just sit watching the engine going round and round, feeling satisfied and proud of my achievement.

Things became a lot worse up at the pen when it was just him and me up there. It was a longer walk now from Cranbrook Street than it had been from Smallshaw and he would go as fast as he could, shouting abuse at me as I lagged behind. But I still wanted to go with him because I was proud that I had a dad who wanted to share his life with me, and I desperately wanted to show him how useful I could be to him.

'Come on, you little bastard, faster.'

Sometimes he would get so far ahead that he would be able to hide in the hedges, particularly on dark evenings, and then jump out at me, frightening me half to death.

'See that moon?' he'd ask, pointing up into the sky. 'He's gonna get you.'

From the time we moved to Cranbrook Street, Granddad from the Pen disappeared, and no one ever explained what had happened to him. I suppose he must have died.

Dad would bully me relentlessly while we were there, treating me like a slave. He would make me fetch water from the well in a bucket that was too big for me to carry. I had to get down on all fours, float the bucket on its side and scoop the water in with my hands, but it would keep on bobbing to the top and not filling up. When I did manage to get some water into it, it would be too heavy for me to carry and its rough edges would bite into my legs as I stumbled back, desperate to please him. Most of the water would have gone by the time I got to him.

'What the fuck is that?' he would demand, before hitting me to the ground. 'Now go and get the fucking water, you useless little bastard!'

Sometimes he would push me into the pig slurry, half pretending he was joking, half punishing me for all my mistakes. It was impossible to remove the smell from my skin once we got home; it became ingrained into me. As well as using the dirty magazines he kept up there, he would also drop his trousers and have sex with the pigs, unbothered whether I saw him. Many years later I discovered he'd let Christina see him as well.

He would force me to do things like kill a chicken, even though my hands were hardly big enough to grip their necks. I so much wanted to please him by doing the jobs he told me to do, but some of them were too frightening.

'I don't want to, Daddy. Please don't make me.'

'Fucking hold it! Put it under your arm, go on, under your arm. Now twist its head, on the neck. Fucking kill it!'

The first time I became hysterical as the giant bird flapped and pecked in my arms. 'You soft cunt,' he said, taking the bird from me, wringing its neck with one easy movement and then punching me to the ground before walking away.

Once he'd killed them he would take them round the pubs to sell them, or down to the market, sometimes taking me with him. To the outside world he showed such a different face to the one we all saw at home. To everyone else he was always laughing and joking, always working, a good husband, father and provider. From his family's point of view he was a good man who had taken on a down-at-heel young Irishwoman and her three kids, one of whom was disabled, taking them from the worst council estate in the area to a private house. No one on the outside ever saw the way he treated us in that private house, or in that fortified pen.

'I could snuff you out like that,' he would sneer, snapping his fingers to show how easily he could dispense with such a worthless piece of rubbish as me.

The Jack Russells were often having litters of puppies, which he would sell around the pubs, but one day he decided on a different course. Christina and I had been playing with them when he came in with a black blanket and threw them into it.

'Come on, Stuart, we're going.'

We went out to the Austin Maxi he drove then and he tossed the blanket containing the puppies on to the floor in front of me. They were squealing for their mother.

'Where are we going?' I asked.

'Up the pen.'

When we got there he took the blanket, untied it and dropped the puppies on my lap. As I played with them and stroked them he fetched a bucket of water. He took each puppy in turn and held it under the water. At first I didn't understand what was going on as he tossed the limp, wet little bodies back into my lap, laughing at the puzzlement on my face. I kept stroking them, not able to take in what was happening. Then he took them, one by one, and hurled them over the hedge. I begged him to stop but he just kept going with a daft smile on his face, mocking me.

When he had puppies he wanted to sell he would cut off their tails with a big pair of scissors, making me cry as loudly as they did. Then he would cauterize the stumps with a red-hot knife from the stove. I suppose some of his actions were the traditional country ways of doing things, lessons he had probably learned from his own father, but I couldn't understand the pleasure he seemed to take in hurting people and animals. On one occasion he castrated Bobby the boar and rubbed the blooded testicles on my face, pretending it was a joke, but not letting me wriggle free until he'd finished. For some reason he hated cats; whenever he saw one he would kick it as hard as he could.

Although I loathed all the things he did to me, he was still my hero, especially when he got himself a gun as part of his continuous campaign against the rats up at the pen. It was a 12-bore and he kept it in the bedroom, along with all the ammunition. I sneaked in there one afternoon to have a look at it. As I gazed at it in wonder, stroking it nervously, I was suddenly aware of his presence behind me.

'What're yer doing?'

'Just looking.' I knew something bad was coming.

'Sit on the bed.' I obeyed, trembling. He levered the gun open and loaded a bright red cartridge. He snapped the gun shut. 'Open yer mouth.'

I was shaking so much my teeth chattered against the barrel as he forced it into my open mouth and held it there, reminding me yet again that he could snuff me out in a second. 'I'm going to kill you now.'

My body twitched and shook, my tears and saliva running over the barrel. After what seemed like an age he withdrew the barrel, looking at me with pure disgust. He hated me and I knew it.

'Now fuck off.'

Chapter Seven

JUST MESSING AROUND

At weekends Dad used to have a gardening job at a big Victorian house on the other side of town. He was always working hard and he taught me the importance of making your own way in the world. Considering how hard he worked, it was strange that he never had any money. I suppose he spent it all in the pub. Work has been a great comfort to me down the years, providing the approval I always wanted to receive from him.

He had his own big gardener's shed at the house, where he used to keep another stash of pornographic magazines and would sit masturbating. I would go with him sometimes and it would make me feel proud to be going to work with my dad, even if he would stride ahead and leave me behind on the way. He would have me picking up leaves or whatever he needed doing, shouting orders and criticisms at me all the time like he hated me.

The lady of the house or her daughter used to bring us out tea and biscuits on a tray and he played the part of the respectful gardener perfectly; they thought he was great. Once they'd gone back into the house he would tell me he was going to go in and give them both 'a shagging'. If he went into the house for any reason he would come back and tell me he'd been 'having a bit'. I hated it when he talked like that to me.

He was becoming more and more sexually explicit with me all the time, almost as if I was his mate, sometimes, rather than his son. He used to like to help the terriers to mate, masturbating Bobby, the dog, to get him excited and making me touch him and Trixie and then sniff my fingers. I would try to look away and he would get angry with me.

'Watch the shagging, you little bastard,' he'd shout as he masturbated himself. 'Watch the shagging.'

I didn't like it and would try to look away.

'Fucking look at it!'

Dad often would masturbate on to the carpet in front of us and then call the dogs to clean up the mess.

At school I was a bit boisterous, but desperate to please everyone. I wanted them all to see that Stuart was a good boy, not a naughty boy. I got myself into the football team and longed for Mum and Dad to come and watch me play, but they never did.

Sometimes in the evenings we would be left with a babysitter. He was a lad from the big family in Smallshaw whose mum had fought with our mum in the street. He and Dad seemed to be close, although I never quite worked out what was going on between them. He used to get into bed with me and then the bed would start shaking, just like with Dad. But it was different from the way Dad went about things – the babysitter would coax me with kindness and sweets and tickling. He didn't seem to want to prove he had power over me like Dad did; he didn't seem to want to hurt me or humiliate me, but he did want to use me to satisfy himself.

Shirley used to be taken swimming at the local baths every so often by some charity helpers, and I was allowed to go with them. The pool was closed to the general public so the disabled kids could have it to themselves for a couple of hours. After one session, when I was five or six, I was in the showers with the two men who had been carrying Shirley around, just the three of us, and they persuaded me to masturbate them. It seemed to me as if every grown man I came across wanted the same thing. I guess kids from dysfunctional families are always going to be easy prey to paedophiles.

When Clare was about a year old I woke up in the night to hear a lot of shouting and screaming going on downstairs. Instantly afraid, I listened to the sounds growing louder and more violent. I heard footsteps running up the stairs and the bedroom door burst open as Mum ran in with Clare in her arms.

'I'm getting in with you,' she said, climbing into my bed.

A few seconds later Christina followed, white-faced and wide-eyed, and curled up at the bottom of the bed, followed by Dad in the purple suit he sometimes wore to go out.

'You fucking slag,' he shouted, reeling into the room, roaring drunk. 'You fucking get back downstairs.'

'No, David,' Mum said, 'I'm not coming downstairs. You really hurt me.' He'd been punching her and now nearly pulled her arm out of its socket as he tried to drag her out of the bed. She clung on desperately. We were all crying, terrified of what would happen next. He gave up trying to pull her out, pushed us over instead and forced himself into the little bed as well.

'I'll stay here then.'

Then he seemed to change his mind. I had a heavy metal clock by the side of the bed, which he'd salvaged from the bins. He climbed off the bed and pulled his sock off, stuffing the clock into it. Standing up he started swinging it unsteadily around like a cosh. He had lurched over by the window and for a second I considered rushing at him and toppling him backwards through it. I knew it would mean I would fall with him, but hopefully I would land on top of him and he would cushion the impact for me.

Panic-stricken, I jumped out of bed as he lunged forward towards Mum with the cosh, and I made a dash for the door. I could feel the warmth of urine trickling down my leg. Christina was on her feet and running too and Dad was right behind us. The bedroom door seemed to take ages to open, but we managed to get through it and started down the stairs. I was forcing my legs to take the steps as quickly as possible, knowing he would kill us if he managed to get his hands on us.

I knew the front door would take even longer than the bedroom door and was sure he would get us there, but he must have stumbled on the way down the stairs because I managed to get the locks open and we were out in the street. It had been snowing and the pavement was like ice under my feet as I ran.

'Daddy's killing us! Daddy's killing us all! Help!' I yelled as I ran, expecting to be grabbed from behind at any moment.

Christina had gone in the opposite direction and to my relief I realized he'd decided to go after her first. I had a few minutes in which to get help. A friend of mine, Gary, lived further up the street and I banged on his door, yelling for help. The moment his dad opened the door I ran in, slamming it behind me, as if there were a pack of wolves snapping at my heels.

'Please, please, you have to help us,' I sobbed hysterically. 'He's killing us all.'

Gary's mum gave me a hug and tried to comfort me as I sobbed and gabbled on about how Dad was going to kill Clare, while Gary's dad went round to the house. They all came back together.

'Don't worry, lad,' Gary's dad tried to reassure me. 'Your mum and dad have explained they were just messing around.'

I was horrified because I could see he believed what he was saying and thought I was wrong. I just wanted to stay safe with Gary's mum. I wanted them to tell someone in authority what was going on in our house. I wanted Mum to admit how bad things were and take this opportunity to get us help. But none of these things happened. The grown-ups closed ranks, all reasonable and concerned and keen to get us back home as quickly as possible. I was terrified what would happen once we were back behind closed doors, but the cold air must have sobered him up because that night they just put us back to bed as if their cover story had been true, that they had just been messing around and had allowed their games to get out of hand. Maybe Dad had realized he had endangered everything by pushing his luck a bit too far. I felt guilty about talking to other people about him and hoped he wouldn't decide to punish me for it the next day.

By the time I was ten I was desperate to earn a bit of money for myself, so that I could at least buy myself something to eat from time to time. There was a milkman who delivered in our area called Stuart. I used to smile at him and he used to wink back, a friendly older man with a beard. One day I asked him if I could help him on his rounds and he said I could. I knew I had to keep it secret otherwise Dad would put a stop to it, and I felt very guilty about deceiving him, but my urge for a little independence was stronger than my fear of the reprisals.

Each morning I would let myself out of the house while everyone was still asleep and run to find Stuart's milk float. He would let me do the running up and down with the bottles and I learned which houses left out money for him to collect. At the end of the round he would give me some money and I would be straight up the shop to buy sweets. I would stuff in as many as I could before I got home, making myself sick in my haste to cram them in, throwing the rest away in case Dad found them and realized what I had been up to without his permission. I loved Stuart the milkman because he would tell me I was a 'good boy', which was all I ever wanted to hear.

It was 1979 and I was eleven years old when I came home one afternoon to find my Auntie June in the kitchen with Mum, Christina and Clare. Mum should have been at work, which was puzzling, and Dad was nowhere to be seen. I could tell something dramatic had happened, it was written all over their faces, and their shock hung in the air like a dark, ominous cloud.

'What's going on?' I asked.

'Your Dad's been messing with the girls,' Mum told me. 'And he's gone.'

'Yeah, but where's he gone?'

'Why don't you go back out and play, Stuart? Me and your Auntie have a few things to talk about.'

I was shocked, even though I had seen things happening and should have guessed that they had gone a lot further when I wasn't around. I suppose I'd been block-ing out the truth, unable to believe that even my dad was such a bad man that he would do such things to innocent girls, especially Shirley, who could do nothing to defend herself and was already suffering a life of relentless pain and boredom.

I went off to pass a few more hours while they talked grown-up talk. I went to a den I'd made in some waste ground at a disused coal pit nearby and began to cry. I wondered what I had done wrong that I should be sent away while they talked. I wanted to know what they were saying. Had they found out I was really bad and naughty? Now that the truth was coming out, would I be put in a home just as Dad was always threat-ening? Would the police come for me? Might I even die? Might Shirley or Clare die? Would Mum leave me? Would they take Christina away from me? There were so many unknowns and each one was more frightening than the last.

Sometimes Dad used to tell Christina and me that Shirley was going to die, so I was always aware of the pos-sibility. He would say that to save Shirley we would have to be good and do whatever he told us. But I hadn't been good. I knew that because he was always telling me so.

Eventually I found out a bit more of what had hap-pened that day while I was at school. Dad had been threatening the girls, making lewd promises about what he was going to do to them next time Mum was out, and Christina finally couldn't stand it any more. When Mum announced she was going out to bingo, the girls begged her not to go.

'Why ever not?' she asked, shocked by the vehemence of their pleading, and then they told her some of what had been going on.

Unable to think clearly, she had gone straight round to get my Auntie June. I guess she felt she needed support in case Dad turned violent when confronted. June was furious with him and stormed back to the house with Mum, going straight up to Dad and slapping his face. Apparently he tried to deny it to begin with, but when they threatened to call the police he confessed. At first he said he had done it to teach them what to do when they were older. Then he said he knew it was wrong and that he didn't know why he did it. Mum sent him away from the house and he left without an argument.

Mum knew how often he battered me around, but she also knew how much I loved him despite all that and how much I wanted him to love me. It never occurred to her that he might have been doing the same to me that he had been doing to the girls. I certainly wasn't going to tell anyone, because if I did they would know that I had been a naughty boy and they would probably take me away to a home. In my muddled young mind what he had done to the girls was different; he had been wrong to punish them, but he had been right to punish me because I was so bad. When I realized that no one was going to find out how bad I'd been I felt relieved, but I still didn't like all the uncertainty, which was now affecting all of us.

Dad moved up to the pen, just like his dad had before him, but he kept coming back to the house, being charming, trying to show that he was sorry and that it would be OK for him to come home because he'd learned his lesson. He asked Mum if he could take Christina and me up to the pen with him, and she said yes. He had a little van at the time, like a box attached to a motorbike really, and he let us both drive it up the lane. I really missed him, even though I didn't miss the batterings and everything else. I was sure he would behave better if he were allowed to come back now. He couldn't go back to his old ways now that he'd been found out, could he?

He started turning up at school like a model father, waiting to pick us up and telling us he was going to be coming home soon. But Mum was adamant she didn't want him back, so when the charm didn't work after a few weeks he returned to his usual bullying and shouting – banging on the door when he was drunk, threatening to kill us all, shoot us and burn the house down. I stayed out of the way as much as I could, just wanting my parents to sort everything out between them like grown-ups should.

One evening I came back from playing football on the local school fields. As I emerged from the ginnel almost opposite our house I saw the front door open and two men came out with Dad. I ducked back out of sight, not wanting to be in any sort of trouble. The men looked official. They walked Dad to a waiting car; one of them opened the back door and when he put his hand on Dad's

head to make sure he didn't bang it as he got in, I realized Dad was handcuffed. I'd seen people being helped
into cars like this on the television news and in police
dramas and I knew it meant he had been arrested.

I was overcome with panic. Did this mean the police
knew everything? Did they know just what a naughty
boy I had been all my life and how often Dad had had to
punish me? If they were taking him away for whatever he
had done, would they be back to take me away as well?
Maybe they would take me away and put me in a home,
just like he had always threatened they would. Not knowing where else to go, I ran to the school playground,
hugged the wall and cried for what seemed like hours.

When I finally went back to the house Mum was sitting in the kitchen. 'They've taken your dad away,' she
said, and I felt overwhelmingly sad. I didn't want my
Dad to be taken away. I didn't want him to go on treating
me the way he had in the past, but I didn't want to lose
him completely.

The courts must have told him he had to stay away
from us until the time of his trial and he went to Wales
to stay with his sister Doris and her husband, Stuart.
Doris had never liked me much, and the feeling was
mutual. She seemed resentful and bitter like Dad, and
used to slipper me at the slightest provocation. But Stuart
was a nice man, another bearded 'Father Christmas' figure.
I had always wished Dad could be more like him. My
cousins, John and Cheryl, I used to love to bits, and we
would play in the fields and the quarries just like normal

children whenever we were together. Dad never abused me during the times we stayed there, when there were other people around. At times like that he would always behave like the perfect, loving father, the one I always wanted him to be. Aunt Doris never believed that Dad had done anything wrong or that anything had gone on between him and the girls. She had never had much time for Mum, and I think she tarred Christina with the same brush, believing that if anything did go on it was because she had wanted it to happen.

Once the truth was out Shirley, Christina and Clare had to go and see doctors and child psychologists to check how much damage he had done to them. But I was pretty much left to my own devices. I ran wild out of the house most of the time. Perhaps the grown-ups thought they were sheltering me from terrible truths by sending me out to play while all the details of what he had done to the girls were being gone over and over. But I knew truths they were only just starting to imagine.

Shirley and Christina were supposed to give evidence at his trial, but Shirley wasn't able to do so because she got too upset and Mum was afraid it would bring on her epileptic fits. Even without Shirley's testimony he was sent away to prison for two years, although he probably would have got much longer if she had spoken up. It never occurred to anyone to ask me if anything similar had happened to me – after all, I was a boy. It confirmed to me that Dad had been wrong in what he had done to the girls, because they had never been naughty like me. I had deserved my punishments, I understood that, and I didn't want everyone to know just how bad I had been for so many years, so I continued to say nothing.

I wanted my dad back, but I didn't want to have to return to living in terror. Mum must have had similar mixed feelings. She started sleeping downstairs and we could hear her crying at night. Even though he was gone, none of us hugged each other or showed any outward signs of how much we loved one another; we'd had all that sort of thing beaten out of us. None of us could trust anyone for fear of getting hurt, not even each other. I didn't know how Mum would react if I did tell her what he had been doing to me all those years. I didn't even know if she would believe me, and I didn't want her to think I was a naughty boy too. So I kept quiet, just as I always had.

'It'll be all right, Mum,' I would say when I found her crying. 'I'll look after you. We'll get through.'

'You're the man of the house now,' she said, giving me a cigarette for the first time. I'd been smoking since I was nine, but never in front of her.

'I know, Mum,' I said, trying to puff on the fag as if it were the most natural thing in the world. I took her words as a challenge. If I were the man of the house, then that meant I would need to be the provider from now on. It made me feel important. She went through all her bills with me, working out the mortgage repayments and the electric bills. There was never enough left over for us to buy food.

'Do you miss your Dad?' she would ask sometimes, and I wanted to tell her everything but I just couldn't.

'There's something you should know,' Mum said one day. 'David's not your real dad. You had the same dad as the girls, George Heywood. But David wanted everyone to think you were his, including you.'

I was devastated. Despite everything he had done to me and to the rest of my family, he had always remained my hero. I had always loved him because he was my dad, but now Mum was telling me even that was a lie. I didn't know whether to believe her or not. She was telling me she had been lying to me all my life about who my father was, but how did I know this wasn't the lie? Maybe he was my father and she just wanted to offer me a more bearable alternative. It felt like my head was going to burst.

Chapter Eight

THE MAN OF THE HOUSE

*E*ven though we had had the daily terror of living with Dad taken away, life was by no means easy. Our dad was in prison, and Mum had to give up work to look after Shirley and Clare, both of whom needed special care in their different ways, so we had virtually no income. The house was falling down around us, the wiring was all knackered and the smell of damp rising up from the cellar gradually infected every floor. It was so cold at night we would wrap ourselves in newspapers and heap all the coats in the house on top of us, and in the morning the insides of the windows would be frozen. The newspapers would leave me grubby with ink, but that was the least of my problems. I was used to looking dirty.

Being head of a family like this would have been a lot for a grown man with a job to take on, never mind an eleven-year-old who had spent most of the last few years being beaten up and sniffing glue. The first problem was getting enough food so we didn't starve. I started robbing bread, milk and potatoes off people's doorsteps, remembering from my days on the milk round which houses to go to, including the ones that left money out under the mat. I didn't feel guilty because I knew we were desperate. We weren't bad people but we were on the verge of starvation and I had to do whatever I could to keep us going; that was now my purpose in life. Stuart the milkman had retired by then, so it didn't seem like anything personal against him. I would have felt bad to steal from his round after he had been so kind.

Some of our food I pinched from our local Presto store, wearing Christina's duffel coat and filling the pockets with beans or whatever else I could get hold of. I'd worked out there was a blind spot in the mirror where they couldn't see what I was up to. But I wasn't as clever as I thought and on one occasion the store detective stopped me.

'I've just seen you nicking chocolate,' he told me. 'What have you got under your coat?'

'Nothing,' I said.

'Hold your arms up.'

I did as he told me and two loaves of bread landed on the floor at my feet. 'It's for me mum,' I said, unable to stop myself from crying. 'Me sister's in a wheelchair and we've got no money.'

He looked at me hard, then bent down and picked up the bread. He pushed it into my hands. 'Go on,' he said, 'get out of here.'

I ran home at full speed, but it wasn't the last time I went shoplifting – it couldn't be, we needed too much.

I might be able to put the odd meal on the table, but I couldn't do anything about our debts. There were always people coming to the door and letters flopping on to the mat, just like it had been in Smallshaw Lane. I got myself a paper round in order to earn some extra money, but it was nothing like enough to keep us afloat.

Mum was beside herself with worry and kept asking us if we wanted our dad to come back to live with us when he was released. He'd started putting requests on the radio from Strangeways for us as a family and had sent home models he'd made from matchsticks, trying to charm us into believing he would be a reformed character. I wanted my dad back, but I didn't want him in the house with us in case he started doing all the same things again. I thought if I could support the family then he would be able to see he wasn't needed. I wanted him to see what a good job I had made of filling his shoes while he was away. I also wanted to show my mum just how much I loved her, even though I could never say it out loud. I was pretty sure she loved me too, although sometimes I got angry when I wondered why she hadn't tried to protect me from him when I was small.

Another source of emergency cash was all the junk that he had brought back to the house over the years, like the swords with the jewels in them, and the brass ornaments. Every weekend I would take something else round the second-hand shops trying to get the best prices possible. I got pretty good at haggling, sometimes visiting the same shopkeeper several times before finally agreeing a price. On the day the swords went a friend and I used them for duelling all the way to the shops. Even if I was now the main breadwinner, I was still only twelve years old.

I discovered that if I joined the local church choir they would pay me two pounds just to turn up. I couldn't sing a note, but I could mime. I also liked jumping up and pulling the ropes that set the church bells ringing, which would also set the vicar shouting at me. I used to love to listen to the stories from the Bible, so much so that the vicar came to see Mum and suggested I might benefit from a bit more religious education, but I was really only there for the money. Most of the other choirboys were from quite well-to-do homes and I didn't fit in at all – I was just a boisterous little urchin running around getting told off all the time.

I joined the Boys' Brigade as well and got to play the bugle and drums and be in their football team. I liked the marching and the uniforms and during the football matches I liked the oranges they brought on at half time. I liked the uniform so much I tried to wear it to school, but that got me into trouble. It was clean and smart and made me feel proud when I wore it, like I was someone important, not just rubbish as Dad had always told me I was. I used to wear it round the house as well.

I would practise the bugle at home and one of the neighbours came knocking at the door one day.

'Is your son musically minded?' he asked.

'Yes, I think he is,' Mum replied proudly.

'Does he enjoy playing that bugle?'

'Yes he does.' Now she was thinking he might be going to donate an old bugle he didn't need any more.

'Well,' the neighbour said, 'tell him if he doesn't stop playing that thing morning, noon and night I'm going to smash it over his fucking head.'

Mum changed jobs and went to work in a fish and chip shop, so some evenings she would bring us back left-over chips. Tina the Alsatian, Bobby and Trixie had gone by then and she had bought herself a border collie to replace them.

With Dad out of the house I finally had a chance at making some friends. I would steal things to give them, to make them like me, and invite them back to the house for company, even though I was embarrassed to have them see the state we were living in. I could see it all through their eyes, with Shirley slumped in her wheel-chair and Clare continually rocking back and forth on the sofa, lost in her own world. I used to take the mick-ey out of Clare myself sometimes, out of embarrass-ment. She would have her music so loud we had to get her a pair of headphones, so the rest of us could hear ourselves think, but she would sing tunelessly along to endless Don Williams Country and Western tracks at the top of her voice, a dreadful wailing sound that filled the house. In the end we banished her to her bedroom but we could still hear her as if she was in the same room, as well as the creaking of the bed as she bounced up and down.

'Are you gay, Stuart?' Mum asked out of the blue one day. 'It's all right if you are.' Why did it make me gay just because I wanted to have some mates stay over when I was twelve and thirteen? I thought it was something normal to do, not something abnormal. I was cross with her because of the things that had been done to me when I was little and because I was worried my friends would overhear her talking. I had never had a gay thought in my life, but I would no more have known how to start a relationship with a girl than fly to the moon. I was interested in girls but I was very afraid of sex, and I suspected every boy I met of being a paedophile. Other boys talked about touching girls the whole time, but they didn't talk about love or any of the romantic stuff. I thought they were all disgusting, just like Dad and Granddad from the Pen with their magazines, the babysitter with his sweets and the men in the showers of the swimming pool.

Although I was the class clown, my teachers were starting to tell Mum that I was very bright. I wanted to be loved and I realized that if I messed around in class and cheeked the teachers a bit it would make the others laugh, which would mean they liked me. But even though I messed about, I was still good in exams and did quite well. I hated myself all the time, because I knew I was bad and I wanted to be good. I would hit myself sometimes, and cut myself, just because I hated me so much. Why did I have to be the person I was? Why did I have to have the dad I did? Why did Christina and I have to share our clothes? I was full of hatred for my whole life and emotionally I stopped developing, frozen as a small, confused, hurt boy, even as my body was growing into a man, a big man. If anyone asked me how I got the bruises I would just say I'd been in a fight. I felt embarrassed, guilty and ashamed of my behaviour but life seemed to have no point. My family was all broken; Mum was always out and the house scruffy and dirty.

I always loved Mum, and wanted her to love me. But none of us knew how to love. There was never any kisses or cuddling. Nobody ever came to watch me in a swimming gala or winning trophies playing football, or even on school sports days when everyone else's parents were there, cheering and waving. We weren't taught how to deal with sadness or anger and there were never any bedtime stories, apart from the ones Christina used to tell me. Fairy tales never existed in our world and no one ever lived happily ever after. I wanted to be cared for and to belong. I wanted the world to be a safe place where there were no demons or monsters. I wanted to fit in, but I never felt I did.

I would lie a lot about Dad, making up stories of how I wanted my life to be rather than how it was. I would tell the other kids I'd been fishing with him at the weekend, or that he'd taken me for a ride in his car.

I started running wild, staying out late, drinking and smoking. There was a warehouse nearby where they stored old cider bottles and a friend and I used to break in at night and drink all the dregs. Then we would steal a few crates of empties and take them back to the shop the next day to claim the refunds. Mum tried to get some control over me, but it was too late by then: she had already told me I was the man of the family. She couldn't expect to be able to take it back and boss me about; she couldn't have it both ways.

I was too fearful of other people to become really violent. I could take a beating without too much trouble, but I couldn't give one out. There was also a part of me that was frightened that if I ever lost control of the rage that I kept bottled up inside me, I might really hurt someone, and I knew what that felt like.

'You blame me, don't you,' Mum would say whenever we fell out, 'for sending your dad away.'

I hated her saying that. Nothing could have been further from the truth. If anything, I blamed her for not doing anything to protect us all those years before.

I could never feel sorry for myself because whenever I did I just had to look at Shirley and realize I had nothing to complain about. Her whole life she'd been stuck in a wheelchair with nothing to do, half her body not working, dependent on others who then abused her, and never knowing when she was next going to have a fit. If she never complained, what right had I got?

Christina seemed to have been more disturbed by what had happened to her than Shirley. We never talked to one another about it, but she was obviously in a terrible state, literally tearing her hair out and smashing things up around the house in her anger and frustration at the hand fate had dealt her. She was becoming a beautiful girl and would eventually do well in beauty competitions, but that didn't make her any happier. Whereas I seemed to survive by bottling my misery up, she let hers rip at full volume. I guess in the long run, considering what would happen when I finally exploded, hers was the healthier option, but at the time it seemed like she was permanently in pain.

As the second Christmas since Dad went to prison approached, I found Mum sitting on the sofa in tears. 'Christmas is always shit,' she said through sobs. 'We've got no money for presents or anything.'

I tried to comfort her, and determined to do the best I could to give us a good Christmas. I felt so sorry for her. No matter what mistakes she'd made she had always managed to keep us together as a family, when many other women would have given up the struggle and had us put into foster care or homes. Even with all Shirley and Clare's problems she had never given up on them. I was sure she had wanted Dad to love her just as much as I had wanted him to love me.

I set off to the toy store in Oldham with a mission. I browsed around the shelves for a while, working out what I wanted and checking out the staff. I noticed that a lot of the other customers were already carrying plastic bags from the same store with purchases they'd made earlier. I waited until all the staff were looking the other way and crept up to the counter and took a bag. Going to the other end of the store, my heart thumping in my chest, I put the stuff I wanted into the bag and walked out the door. Nobody stopped me. I got all the way home and stashed the toys in my walk-in wardrobe. I'd got away with it and felt very pleased with myself. Dad had never been able to give us a good Christmas, but I was going to.

I took the same bag back twice more with equal success, but what I hadn't noticed on the third trip was that Jim, Mum's collie, had chewed the corner of the bag. The manageress, however, spotted a boy with a chewed carrier bag and guessed I hadn't just made a purchase. The moment she called me back into the shop and accused me of shoplifting I burst into tears. I was never far from tears, always living on a nervous edge. I blurted out my story about my sisters being abused and one of them being in a wheelchair, which usually got a sympathetic reaction, but she wasn't interested. She rang the police and I was taken to the station and charged.

Mum was convinced I'd done it to get back at her for sending Dad to prison, but it was nothing like that. I had just wanted to give us a good Christmas for once. The magistrate put me under a supervision order, and no one else knew about the toys from my other missions, which were already safely hidden in my wardrobe. On Christmas Eve I made Mum promise she wouldn't shout at me if I told her a secret. I couldn't bear being shouted at by anyone – raised voices bringing back terrible memories and making me tremble with fear and anticipation of pain. She promised and I showed her the presents I'd got for us. Instead of shouting and being angry she just cried, and the next day I felt proud of myself for having been able to provide the best Christmas we'd ever had as a family.

Chapter Nine

NO ANSWERS

I didn't want Dad to come back and live with us when he came out, but I did want to see him again. Despite all the bad things he'd done to me he had taken me everywhere with him and I wanted to have that part of my dad back. I wanted a role model, someone to look up to, someone to protect me, someone to teach me. I wanted him to tell me he loved me, that I wasn't a naughty boy and that I'd done well to look after the family while he was away. I wanted to hear him say that he was proud of me. I wanted him to say he was sorry for the ways in which he'd hurt me. I wanted him to tell me that it wasn't true what Mum had told me, that he was my real Dad.

I thought all that would happen now I was the 'man of the family' and he had served his sentence, that we would be able to start our father–son relationship afresh. I felt I needed a dad, like all the other kids at school, whose dads had been standing on the sidelines when they played cricket and in the school hall when they won prizes.

Because we had said we didn't want him back when he came out of prison, he went to live with his sister Doris in Wales. Once I knew he was there I rang, and I can still remember their telephone number by heart, even now. They agreed I should go to visit and I caught a train down through Llandudno to their local station. When I got there, there was only my cousin, John, waiting for me, so we walked to the house together, with me trying hard to hide my nerves. I was really pleased to see John. We had always had a real bond, like true friends.

Auntie Doris had got a log fire going and Dad was there in her sitting room like it was the most normal thing in the world. He didn't look any different at all, but I must have changed a lot in those two years. I felt a tremendous love for him.

I was to share John's bedroom, with me on the top bunk and him on the bottom; Dad was going to be in there too, on a camp bed. I thought I would be pretty safe on the top, as long as John was there. Dad had never done anything to me when anyone other than Mum or my sisters was around. Over the weekend John and I spent a lot of time together and I didn't really get any time to speak to Dad.

On the second night John and I had gone up to bed together and he was making me laugh by rocking his head around and making himself dizzy. Suddenly the door burst open. Doris exploded into the room with her slipper and gave me a good whacking. After two years of not being touched or physically hurt it unleashed a thousand terrible memories and feelings and I started to cry. The more I cried the more John laughed, because he was used to being slippered and thought nothing of it. The pain of the slipper was nothing compared to what I had been used to, but the pain of the memories it brought to the surface was almost unbearable.

Doris stormed back downstairs, leaving me sobbing. When I eventually calmed down and regained some control I could hear her and Dad talking downstairs: 'I thought he knew he wasn't your lad,' she was saying.

Mustering all my courage, still stinging from her blows, I climbed off the bunk and went downstairs, telling myself I was a grown-up now, the acting head of the family, not wanting to be intimidated by them any longer. Doris was standing by the fire and Dad was on the sofa.

'Are you really me dad?' I asked.

'Of course I'm yer dad.'

'No, but are you *really* me dad?'

"Course he's yer dad,' Doris said, obviously impatient with my nonsense. 'Now go an' get back in bed.'

I did as she instructed, not wanting to risk another outburst from either of them. The next day I left, having had none of my questions answered, and not having heard any of the things that I longed to hear.

I went back again a few weeks later, and ended up spending all my time playing with John again. I was determined not to give up and tried once more a few weeks later. By this time Dad had moved out of Doris's house into a flat above a shop, sharing with a big bearded guy called Peter. Dad had started working for the council again on cleansing. It didn't seem to bother him that I was coming to visit, but it didn't seem to interest him much either.

On the second evening I was there Dad was in the shower and Peter suggested he and I went to the pub to play some pool.

'I don't want to go out,' I said. 'I want to spend some time with my dad.'

'Your dad's got someone coming round,' Peter said.

'What do you mean?'

'We'll just have a game of pool and then come back after.'

There was a knock at the door before I could ask any more and a girl came in. She looked about fifteen, dark haired with glasses. Confused, I went out with Peter and once we were clear of the house I asked who she was. 'She's a prostitute,' he said, matter-of-factly.

I was shocked and disgusted, but I couldn't think what to say. I went along with Peter and by the time we got back to the flat the girl had gone and Dad was in the kitchen having a cup of tea and a roll-up. I wanted to ask him all the questions that were building up in my mind about what he thought of me, but he just kept talking about how he'd been stabbed in prison and I lost my nerve. I was still too terrified of him to say anything that might make him angry.

Eventually, with a surge of courage, I managed to interrupt. 'Why did you hurt Shirley and Christina and do those things to them?'

He immediately started shouting and denying everything, saying it was all a 'pack of lies'. There was no reasoning with him, and there was no chance I would get up the courage to ask why he had done the things he'd inflicted on me. That night I went home again on the train, realizing it was hopeless, that he was never going to be the dad I craved and there was no point hoping for it any longer. I decided I wasn't going to see him any more.

Mum did get a boyfriend for a bit, but I was not happy about it. He was a perfectly nice man, but I was jealous, feeling it was my place to be the man of the family, and I didn't trust any man. When he came round I would sit between them, saying things like, 'What do you want?' all aggressively. I was so scared that if any man got his feet under the table he would start behaving like Dad and would hurt Mum and the girls. I'd become very controlling, always needing to know everything that was going on with everyone in the family, terrified of any strangers who tried to get into our little world. I didn't like uncertainty because I felt that could lead to danger. The man tried hard but I sensed there was something dodgy about him, and it turned out he was seeing another woman at the same time. Women like my mum never seem to have any luck with the men they attract.

By this time the house was completely knackered. The roof was leaking, the kitchen units were falling off the walls, the carpets were rotting, the walls were damp, even the beds were collapsing. There was rubbish every-where, including a pile of old papers, which we used to chuck beside the stairs.

'Sometimes I wish the whole place would catch on fire,' Mum used to say, 'then the insurance would sort us out.'

I brooded on her words. The upstairs was the worst, with no lights or heating apart from one lamp on the stairs, and it occurred to me that if there was a fire we would be able to get it all rewired, mended and decorat-ed. I started to lay plans as to how I might make it con-vincing. On the morning that I finally decided to act I was the last to leave the house. Mum had gone to work, Shirley and Clare were at their special schools and Christina had already gone out. I put a match to the pile of papers, shocked by how quickly and ferociously they started to burn, and ran out of the house. I got to school, found the register sitting on a trolley and signed myself in, then went to class as normal.

In my head I rehearsed how I would explain what had happened. There was a dodgy light switch on the wall that could have blown out and sent sparks on to the newspapers below. There was also the lamp on the land-ing, on a long lead, and the towel that we would hang over the banister to dry, both of which could have played their part. All these stories were spinning round and round in my head as I waited for something to happen. It seemed odd that life was just carrying on as normal in the classroom when I knew what was happening just a couple of streets away. Finally someone called the teacher out and she came back in looking grave.

'Stuart,' she said, 'have you got a minute?'

In the corridor outside was a social worker, whom I had recently been assigned.

'There's been a fire in your house,' he said, and to my horror I started laughing out of sheer nerves. I went back into the classroom.

'Gotta go,' I said cheerily. 'Me house has just burned down.' They all laughed, because I was known as the class clown and they thought I was joking.

As soon as I saw Mum outside the house I realized one thing I had overlooked – the dog! Luckily, it had escaped the moment the fire brigade had gone in, but the thought that I might have cooked Mum's beloved pet made me feel sick. I told the social worker that I wanted to see what had happened, because the fire brigade had made it safe by then. I was shocked by the amount of damage I had done. As well as the wood panelling on the stairs, there were polystyrene tiles on the ceilings and they had carried the fire everywhere. Our bedrooms on the top floor were gutted. Everything was blackened by the smoke and the windows were all cracked and broken – it was like walking through an alien landscape. For some reason I hadn't expected such devastation.

The family of one of my friends from one door down the road agreed to take us in until we were able to find somewhere new for ourselves. The problem was what to do with Shirley because she needed so much help and attention and there just wasn't room for her in another family's house. The council suggested moving her into a home called Catherine House, where she could have her own little self-contained flat.

Our neighbours were great, but there was a limit to how long we could impose on them, and the council soon moved us to a battered wives' refuge, The Twelve Apostles, where we had our own third-floor flat, with a great view out over the city skyline. It was a very basic place, but clean and warm. The worst thing about it was the men who would come hammering on the doors late at night, shouting for their wives and kids, their voices ugly and frightening from a mixture of anger and drink, and reminding us of all the rows we'd overheard in our childhoods.

The fire officer came to see Mum about Cranbrook Street. 'I can't understand how the fire started,' he said. 'Would you mind coming up to the house with me?'

'Can I come, Mum?' I jumped in, eager to make sure he saw all the possible ways it could have started.

The moment we got there I immediately started babbling on with all the possible theories I had devised in my head. I could see them both looking at me a bit oddly but I couldn't help myself from waffling on about light switches and sparks.

'Will you just be quiet for one minute, Stuart,' Mum said, obviously exasperated by my hyperactivity. I don't know if the fire brigade ever solved the mystery; I never heard any more about it.

After about three months the council found us a house of our own in an area called Platting Grove. It was semi-detached, built with sheets of grey concrete, in an estate of identical houses. They all belonged to the council at that stage so there was no individuality, no gardens or fences or gates, just the bare necessities. I don't know what happened with the insurance in the end, but I know we never got enough money together to move back into the house. We stayed put in our new council home and I dare say Mum was relieved to be free of the mortgage repayments.

Shirley decided she didn't want to come back and live with us. She was seventeen and it seemed like a good time for her to start being a bit more independent of the family, not that she would ever have been able to live on her own without helpers to lift her around. Catherine House was supposed to be a temporary arrangement, just until we were set up to take her back, but once she got there, and started meeting boys, and particularly one boy, Wayne, who also had spina bifida, she decided she wanted to stay.

It was just the opportunity she needed to escape from her terrible childhood. When you are as poor as we were, it is impossible to give someone as handicapped as Shirley a decent life, no matter how much the government might try to make it possible. Add to that all the horrors she had had inflicted on her, or had had to witness, at the hands of our dad and you could see why Catherine House was able to offer her so much more, with their outings and all the other people there, and her trips to college. She had her own little kitchen where she could brew up for herself, and no stairs she could fall down. She finally got to do some amazing things like canoeing, pot-holing, gliding and going abroad, instead of just sitting in our front room year after year, watching us all fighting to survive and hardly ever going outside.

Our whole family was struggling with insecurities. Christina, who was sixteen by then, found it hard to build relationships with boys, always being jealous and possessive. In many ways she had taken on the role of mother in the house, even though she was still at school. She also seemed to have developed a terrible hatred for Mum, blaming her for everything that had gone wrong in our lives and accusing her of never wanting to have Shirley there. They were always rowing, with Christina crying, hitting herself and locking herself away in her room. 'I was the one who brought her up, not you,' she would rant. 'You never cared about any of us.' She was also unable to refer to Dad as anything other than 'it'.

I was drinking more and starting to use magic mushrooms, anything to dull the pain of being me for a few hours at a time, distracting myself from the reality of my life. Mum had got herself a job behind a bar in the local pub, which meant Clare was left alone a lot of the time, just sitting and rocking and listening to Don Williams, or going upstairs and walking endlessly back and forth in her bedroom for hours at a time. She comforted herself continually with chocolate. Any suggestions on things she might do to help herself were rejected. 'Leave me alone,' was all she would say, and so we did. She seemed unable to tell us what she wanted, existing in a world of her own. Each day a taxi would come to transport her to a special school, just like Shirley, but whenever she was at home she just did the same things, over and over again.

I began to get interested in girls at school, but I was uncomfortable about sex. I wanted to give them pleasure, but I didn't think I should receive any. If any girl tried to touch me I would push her away, accusing her of being a 'filthy slag'. My feelings and urges and memories and fears had all become so entangled it was impossible to work out what I really felt or wanted. As a result the girls thought I was a really nice guy, but they also knew I was totally different to the other boys. They liked the way that I had a soft side, wanting just to hug and cuddle and be close, things we had never been able to do as a family. Once I was going out with them I wanted to be with them every second of the day. Just like Christina I became jealous and possessive. I started smoking weed for a while, trying to chill out a bit.

There was a handyman working up at Catherine House, driving the minibus and taking the residents swimming, whom Mum started going out with. Then he left his job and was replaced by another guy called Tim, whom I quite liked because he was good with Shirley. He also took over going out with Mum. One day I came walking home from school towards the house in Platting Grove and I heard some noises. It took me a moment to realize they were emanating from Mum's open bedroom window, and that they were the sounds of two people having very vocal sex. I felt a surge of disgust, remembering all the vile things I'd been made to do and had had done to me over the years.

'You fucking, dirty slag,' I screamed up at the window. 'The whole fucking street can hear you!'

I went in through the front door, slamming it shut behind me, but the noises carried on upstairs, echoing round the house, taunting me. I just wanted the noises to stop and I screamed, overcome with panic and hysteria, 'Pack it in! Stop it, you dirty bastards!'

Tim suddenly came crashing down the stairs towards me, grabbed me by the throat, threw me against the wall and started strangling me. We struggled for a few moments before breaking apart and I stormed out of the house, desperate to get away from the whole scene, which reminded me so vividly of my childhood and my father. The sex and the violence and the anger all mixed together, leaving me frightened and disgusted. I didn't go home that night, or the next, preferring to sleep rough on some nearby waste ground, too terrified and repulsed to be able to go back.

After a while that relationship petered out as well, and a couple of years later we discovered that Tim had had a relationship with an ex-patient from Catherine House, in a flat a few streets away from us. There was an item on the news one night, with a body being carried out of the flat. Tim was arrested and charged with murdering the woman. He was accused of strangling her and was con-victed of 'unlawful killing'. I realized I'd had a narrow escape that afternoon.

Chapter Ten

MY ROCK

*I*n 1984 Dad met a woman called Barbara Hayward, which was a pretty amazing coincidence considering Mum's name was Heywood when he met her. He met Barbara on his bin round, when he used to stop and chat to her. She had three children from her previous marriage, two boys aged fourteen and four and a girl of ten. A few weeks after they started seeing each other he moved into their council house. So far the pattern could hardly have been more similar. They married two years later and Dad tried to persuade the kids to allow him to adopt them, but they refused. He did, however, persuade Barbara to become pregnant and she later said that their marriage started to break down from that moment onwards.

Their son, Alex, was born in the summer of 1988, twenty years after me. In 1994 Dad was charged with causing actual bodily harm to Alex, who was five by then, and to his older brother, Daniel, who was thirteen.

I hate to think what he may have been putting them through before he was stopped. The marriage split up at that point, having lasted ten years, which was the same length as his relationship with Mum. Dad immediately lost interest in them; no maintenance, no birthday cards, no Christmas presents.

When I came out of school at sixteen, with some decent exam results, I was being a pretty good lad. I smoked a bit of pot, but that was about as bad as it got. I would visit Shirley regularly in her new home. The business with her boyfriend Wayne hadn't worked out because his family had moved him away. They were quite well-to-do and I think they thought he could do better than Shirley, but she was still very happy there, much happier than she had ever been at home. Whenever I felt a bit down, she was my rock. We knew we loved each other, although we never said it, because none of us would ever have said such a thing, and we certainly would never have touched one another affectionately. But we did know how we felt. We could laugh and joke and I would tell her off sometimes if she was being miserable because she would listen to me. I called her 'Shirl the Whirl'.

Even though it was better than home, I felt sorry for her sometimes at Catherine House because many of the other inhabitants were mentally handicapped and she often seemed bored. There were a number of accidents around the home, one of which resulted in Shirley burning herself on an iron because the ironing board was too high; another left her badly scalded when water from a boiling kettle fell in her lap and just lay there because she couldn't feel anything. She was getting very irate and vocal about it all, threatening to sue them for negligence.

'An architect came round to look at the place,' she told me on one visit. 'He said the place had been designed for a "standard disabled person". I asked him what a standard disabled person looked like and he didn't have any answer to that.'

Even though she was starting to fall out with them and believed they were picking on her, she got a lot of good out of Catherine House. The home was involved in a lot of charity work and whenever they needed a spokesperson to accept a cheque or have a picture taken for the papers, they nearly always asked Shirley to do it. All she wanted was to have a job.

'I want to be a receptionist somewhere,' she would tell me. 'Answering the phone, doing some typing. That would do for me.'

I would encourage her to get down the job centre and just sit there till they gave her something, but it wasn't really that easy. I knew how people would look at her and talk to her in public because I'd seen it myself when we all used to go out together as children. Even well-meaning people would talk to her as if she was an imbecile, just because she was in a wheelchair.

'Are you all right, dear?' they would enquire.

'Yeah, I'm fine,' she would reply. 'It's my legs that are damaged, not my head.'

Sometimes as a child I would see people staring at her and I would stick my tongue out and tell them to 'fuck off'.

In a way she knew more about my past than anyone because she had always been there, sitting quietly in the corner of the room in her wheelchair, just taking in everything that went on around her, and she knew what Dad was like. Mum and Christina knew as well, of course, but they were busy getting out and about and on with their lives. Whenever I needed to find an anchor in life it was Shirley I went back to, knowing she would always be there, always the same, always pleased to see me. She was my rock, although I'm sure she never realized it. Seeing how stoical she was about her life would always give me the kick up the arse that I needed, a reminder that any troubles I might have were nothing compared with what she had to go through.

I started to find work and went out with a couple of girls, although both times I became very jealous and possessive again. I could never understand why any girl would be interested in someone as bad and worthless as me. I enjoyed the sex, although I was still a bit afraid of it.

Mum's next boyfriend was Trevor, who was divorced with two kids. He was a big guy, but not intimidating, and I liked him. He was always in the pub when Mum was there but I noticed he would be helping her. When he eventually moved in with us I was pretty difficult, jealous of the love and affection she was showing him when I wasn't getting any. But Trevor was a good man. He had a job and a car and he worked out a bit. He would run us down to visit Shirley, and take her out places. He was always softly spoken, no shouting and no violence.

I was pretty much pleasing myself, staying out too late and smoking too much pot. Mum kept telling me that I had to straighten myself out or get out of the house, but I just saw that as more evidence she was putting Trevor before me, increasing my sense of isolation and unhappiness, making me want to do more bad things. One day I was in the kitchen and Mum and I were arguing about Trevor. My anger boiled up and I threw a plate down on the floor, shattering it. I stood up and stormed over to the door, smashing my head through it. The only trouble was, I couldn't get it back out again, a shard of wood having jammed into my neck. Trevor had to cut me out with his tool kit. On another occasion I punched through the glass of the front window. It was like the anger and resentment bottled up inside me would just erupt every so often.

'You're like a ticking time bomb, Stuart,' Mum would say. 'I never know what's going to happen with you.'

When Christina was seventeen she met an Italian man called Seb, who was about thirty. He was a good-looking guy and manager of the local swimming baths. I liked him right from the start and we became good friends. Even though I was worried about the age gap to begin with, he soon reassured me and I could see he was good with her, even when she sometimes gave him a hard time with her insecurities. Christina fell pregnant at eighteen and they got married, but she suffered terribly from both pre-natal and post-natal depression. For a while she became very unbalanced and told Seb some of the things Dad had done to her as a child. One night she went wandering off in the snow, saying she could hear Dad calling for her; on another occasion she ended up on all fours, barking like a dog. Seb wanted me to give him Dad's address.

'That man has ruined my wife and my family,' he told me over a drink. 'I want you to tell me where to find him.'

But I wouldn't tell him. Part of me still loved my dad, despite everything he had done, and I felt I needed to protect him.

The first job I did was as an engineer, which I didn't really enjoy, standing in one place cutting the same bits of steel all day long. I went to college and did a sheet-metalworker apprenticeship. Then I joined a firm of steeplejacks as an estimator and really took to the work. They gave me a company car and for the first time in my life I felt important. The firm was involved with lightning protection for buildings as well as repairing high chimneys. Whenever I went for any sort of interview I would always do the most enormous amount of research on the subject beforehand, going to libraries, reading books, putting together presentations. I always wanted to impress everyone with what a good boy I was. As a result of all my hard work I excelled at the job and started to get recognized. I had seen how hard Dad had always worked, so I knew what had to be done, and I was terrified of falling into the poverty trap that had engulfed my parents.

When I was eighteen I met a girl called Angela out walking her dog. She was still only sixteen, a lovely girl with long dark hair. I knew her by sight, and knew where she lived. We got talking and became a couple almost there and then. A lot of our early courtship was spent round at Christina and Seb's house, trying to sort things out, like the time Christina went for him with a knife, or the time she smashed a bottle over his head, and scratched his face.

It wasn't until Seb was injured in a motorcycle accident, and I was standing beside his bed in intensive care, looking at all the tubes going in and out of him, that I realized how much I loved him. I stroked his hair, telling him how much we all cared about him and how he must fight to survive. He's told me since that he could hear my voice, even though he couldn't respond. His last request before he lost consciousness was that they didn't cut off his legs, because he lived for his sport, but sadly they were only able to save one of them.

Although I wasn't as out of control as Christina, I was still insecure and possessive, and a bit pathetic at times in my relationship with Angela. But overall I was happy, because I was successful at work. I put my all into it and my efforts were recognized. When I wasn't at work I was going out and enjoying myself, a bit wild at times, one of the lads, and I actually managed to push the memories of my childhood to the back of my mind most of the time. Occasionally I would have a flash of a memory, or a bad dream would wake me up in the night, but I felt I was in control of it. I never talked to Angela about anything that had happened and only very occasionally mentioned to other people that I had been abused as a child, without going into any detail – usually when I'd had a few too many drinks. I still didn't know for sure if Dad was my real dad, or whether it was George Heywood, the same as the girls, and he was just my stepdad, but I was too busy getting on with my life to brood on it any more – I made sure of that.

I was offered a management job up in Scotland and I took it, seeing it as a way to move up in the world, even though it meant Angela and I were apart a lot, which I didn't like. Above anything else I wanted my bosses and my customers to love me, to recognize that I was good at my job, and to that end I was willing to travel to the ends of the earth. Not having any friends or social life in Scotland meant I was able to concentrate on work while I was up there, putting in even more hours than I had before the move. On one of my weekends home Angela announced that she had something to tell me. With my usual insecurity, I thought she was going to want to talk about our relationship and what was wrong with it. She took me upstairs to the bedroom and put her arms around me. I could see my face in the wardrobe mirror over her shoulder as she told me she was pregnant. There was a big smile on my face, but I felt very afraid; how could someone who was still a little boy inside possibly be a good father to a new baby?

Angela's parents believed everything should be done properly and set about organizing the wedding. We were happy to leave it to them as our time was taken up with finding a house in Scotland. I was always a bit jealous around Angela and her father because he hugged her a lot, and because of my twisted upbringing I would wonder what he was after and what might have happened in the past. There were always so many thoughts rushing around in my head that I knew I must never share with anyone else because they were dirty and shameful. I hated myself for having them. I was terrified of saying anything to Angela that might lead to her rejecting me. I couldn't have stood any more rejection.

The wedding day was so organized I just turned up at the church where I had played the bugle a few years before and it was sorted. I was very proud to see that Shirley was there. It poured with rain outside the church and the wind filled the Rolls-Royce with leaves as we made our exit as a married couple. When we got to the restaurant where a meal had been booked we discovered the owner had done a runner with all our money so there was no food or champagne. After the ceremony we went back to Scotland, to our little house, which we didn't have enough money to furnish.

In 1989 Angela gave birth to our son, Matthew, in a little local hospital. I got to bath him about five minutes after he was born and it was without doubt the happiest day of my life up to that point.

'I will always look after you and protect you,' I promised as I gently washed and dried his tiny, helpless, pink little body. I was so in awe of him and instantly loved him.

I might have been a father and husband now, but I was still living on the edge of an emotional precipice. Angela was breastfeeding and usually had Matthew in bed with her once we got home, so in the following months I wasn't feeling as loved and nurtured as I wanted to be. One night I felt so sad and lonely I just took a bottle of rum that we'd had sitting around the house and drank it down. All I remember is sitting at the top of the stairs in our brand new, empty house, throwing up and crying for my mum. If there was ever a time when I told Angela a few of the secrets from my past, that was it, but I have no memory and I have never dared to ask her. I was still only twenty-two years old.

I didn't like living in Scotland and I would come back down to Manchester at every opportunity. If I were on my own I would go out with the lads, and even if I came back with Angela she would stay with her parents and I would stay with my mum. I wanted to be having a good time, afraid I was missing out on life on all the nights Angela and I just stayed in with the baby. When I went out I would deliberately get drunk, because that way I could have a laugh and drown out all the voices and pictures in my head. If I allowed myself to sit still for too long and didn't keep busy I wasn't able to stop the memories from returning. When I slept they returned in the form of nightmares.

After a fairly miserable year in Scotland, not having any friends, we moved back down to Stoke-on-Trent and I started working for a new company, setting up a new division for protecting structures against lightning. We bought an idyllic house, a bungalow with dormer windows in the loft and a nice garden. On the surface things looked as if they were going well, but I was still putting my work before everything, always leaving home at six in the morning and not getting back till nine at night. I felt I was really achieving something on my own, starting with a plain sheet of paper and building something up from nothing.

I was in a meeting with my team one day, briefing them about the jobs they were working on, when Angela called from home, something she hardly ever did.

'What are you doing?' she asked.

'I'm working,' I said, puzzled as to why she would need to ask.

'You'd better stop now and come home.'

'I can't come home now,' I protested. 'I've got all the steeplejacks in the office and we're sorting out the jobs.'

'Stuart,' she said quietly, 'your Shirley's died.'

Her words seemed to unleash every demon I had been keeping so carefully caged inside my head. I felt the same jolt of electricity and heard the same buzzing that I had experienced so often as a child when fear and misery and pain had all descended on me at the same time. There was nothing I could do to keep my emotions under control as I thought about poor Shirley and her miserable life. I shook and cried helplessly as the other men left me in the room to be alone with my grief, having no idea how to cope with the terrible sight and sound of a grown man falling to pieces in front of them. But I didn't feel like a grown man, I felt like a little boy and I wanted to run back to the same playground I had spent so many years in as a child, and hug close to the wall for safety and comfort.

Walking like a man in a trance, I went out to my car, determined to get to Shirley as quickly as possible to see if it was true. I don't remember anything about that journey except that there was a song by Oleta Adams playing on the radio, 'Get Here', and it sounded like Shirley calling to me.

I do remember arriving at Catherine House, walking straight into her room and seeing the empty wheelchair. I sank down on the bed and stared at it. At that moment I knew it was true, that she had gone.

Shirley had drowned in her bathtub. She was still in there; the staff were waiting for the police to come and check for foul play because there was blood in the water, but it turned out to be menstrual. She had been lifted in by a helper at seven thirty that morning, to get her ready for college. The routine was that they would come back every so often to check on her, warm the water up and then lift her out when she was ready. At some stage between these visits she had had a fit and slid under the water, unable to save herself.

I could feel the anger boiling up inside me and I had nowhere to direct it. I went to a pub and started drinking lager. I thought about everything else that had gone wrong in my life. Just a year or so earlier my best friend at the time, Mark, had been killed in a car crash. It had been a colossal shock. The feelings I had been able to control over Mark's sudden death now mixed with my anger over Shirley's. Was everyone I ever cared about going to be taken away from me like this? Was nothing safe or secure? All the fears I had experienced as a small, battered boy swept over me and I couldn't see how I could keep going.

I thought about Dad and all the things he had done to harm us. If it hadn't been for him I would never have started the house fire and Shirley would never have gone into Catherine House. I couldn't understand why everything in my life had to be such shit, and I considered killing myself. Without a thought for Angela or Matthew, I went back to my car and drove to a local beauty spot, high on a hill, looking down over miles of countryside, not another soul in sight. Climbing out of the car I looked up and started shouting at the heavens.

I had found someone to blame. I screamed every name I could think of at him. I wanted to hit someone but there was no one there.

'Why didn't you take me? You had no right to take her. She's been through so much pain and suffering! What purpose does my life have now? How am I going to survive without her?'

All the pictures I had been storing away in boxes in my head came rushing to the front of my mind at once, and through it all I could see poor Shirley, grim-faced and long-suffering, sitting in her wheelchair in the corner of our sitting room while all the horrors of our childhood unfolded around her like a nightmare. At least Christina and I had been able to get up and walk away from time to time, but she had never been able to escape from her personal nightmare, not even for a moment, always reliant on other people for every tiny thing. That night I couldn't sleep and just lay in bed, shaking, remembering things I hadn't thought about for years, like Dad making me abuse the dogs with him. The pictures kept coming into my head and I couldn't get rid of them.

Dad sent Mum a five-pound note, telling her to buy Shirley some flowers.

Chapter Eleven

A TIME BOMB

hirley's death seemed to unbalance all the blocking mechanisms I had built up over the years to keep myself going through the hard times, as if a dam had been dynamited and every memory, every pain and every emotion was flooding through the resulting hole. It felt like everything had changed for me and I was no longer able to keep any control over my life.

I started going to the pub regularly to try to numb the pain with drink. At the funeral I carried her coffin but I wasn't able to cry, even though I wanted to. Afterwards I went to the pub and the tears finally flowed. The girl behind the bar said how sorry she was; everyone in our area knew Shirley because they'd seen her being pushed around in her wheelchair for so many years. A guy sitting at the bar wanted to know what the matter was, why I was crying. I wasn't in the mood to chat with a stranger, so I told him I'd just buried my sister and suggested he kept quiet. But he wouldn't leave it alone.

He told me he had asbestosis and to stop feeling sorry for myself.

'Do you mind,' I said again. 'I've just buried my sister.'

'Fuck your sister,' he snapped.

All of a sudden all my rage came roaring to the surface. I launched myself at him and gave him a terrible battering, having to be restrained by several other people before I did him a serious injury. An ambulance had to be called, and the police came, and I was just sat upstairs, crying and saying how sorry I was. It was as if I had reached the end of my tether; I could no longer cope with the effort needed to stay in control of my anger and my misery and my confusion.

I started going back to places like the dens where I used to sniff glue, just so that I could be on my own, and I would talk aloud to myself, unable to talk properly to anyone else. Looking back now I can see that I was having a nervous breakdown.

Not everything in my life was bad. My bond with Matthew was getting stronger every day. I used to love it when I got in from work and he would be sitting on the windowsill looking out for me. He would rush over to cuddle me, gushing with unconditional love: 'Daddy's here! Daddy's here!'

Sometimes, if he had done something naughty Angela would use me to threaten him. 'Wait till your father gets home,' she would warn. 'Go on, tell Daddy what you did today.'

I begged her not to do that. I wanted him to love me. I didn't want him ever to be frightened or to dread seeing me. Luckily he was such a good boy she hardly ever had to tell him off. Although I had a great relationship with him, I knew he was closer to Angela, after all she was with him most of the time and she had breastfed him and bonded with him. I felt quite jealous and left out sometimes, and Angela seemed never to like to be parted from him, even if it was just for him and me to spend some time together. Sometimes I would come home late and they would be asleep in the same bed and I would have to go to the spare room. I felt very rejected at times like that, but guilty at the same time for coming home so late and not giving them more of my time.

I was always buying Matthew presents; I couldn't go out with him without coming home with some huge new thing for him, like a truck or a remote-controlled car or a tool set, which would exasperate Angela. I wanted him to have stuff that he would enjoy, not like the rubbish Dad would scavenge from the bins for us. I wanted to please him all the time, make him happy, and make him love me. I used to let him smack me on the head with the plastic hammer from his tool kit. One day I'd left my own tool kit out and he picked up the real hammer. Thinking he would be able to make me laugh as usual he came up beside me as I was watching telly and cracked me over the head with it. I buckled up with a scream, sending him scurrying away to hide, suddenly frightened by the unexpected reaction. It was lucky he didn't do me a serious injury. I felt terrible for having frightened him by screaming.

I always wanted to protect him. I would constantly tell him that he mustn't let anyone touch him or look at him, that it 'wasn't right'. I didn't even like it if there were other people around when Angela was changing him as a baby. When I was in the bathroom with him I would even worry about whether that was wrong. It was all such new territory. When we were tiny, Christina and I used to bath together. But Dad would spy on us, and one day he overheard us talking about looking at each other's private parts. He used it as an excuse to get angry with us and to talk about personal stuff, which led to other things as always. So I felt guilty about enjoying bath time with Matthew, dirty by association.

There were so many conflicting messages fermenting in my mind. With Angela I felt I should always give her pleasure in order to show her I loved her. I didn't want to give myself pleasure because that would be dirty, but Dad had taught me that you should do it a lot if you cared about someone. Sometimes Angela would do something to please me and I would scream at her and call her a slag, telling her to get off my back, or whatever the trigger had been. Everything was twisted in my mind and I just couldn't untangle the wrong from the right, the truth from the lies.

Angela's mother was a receptionist at a hospital with access to the phones and so she used to call Angela every day. I would get quite frustrated trying to get through sometimes. I liked to phone home, sometimes as many as twenty times a day, to check they were OK since I was often quite a long way away on a job. I felt guilty about leaving her alone in the house for so long. I knew I could never have stood it, being alone all day with my thoughts. Sometimes I would have so much trouble getting through I would end up phoning the hospital to ask her mother to hang up so I could get through to my own home phone.

All the stress was coming through in other areas of my life and I fell out with my bosses. Knowing that I was good at the job I immediately went into business for myself with a couple of partners, setting up an office in Nottingham and travelling all over the country again. If I kept myself busy every hour of the day I could at least keep the memories and bad thoughts at bay, distract myself with activity and prove my worth by being successful. I worked hard simply to win the approval of those around me. It felt fantastic to set off in the morning in my suit and tie, with my company car and my mobile phone, something that very few people had at that date. I was employing about twenty people, many of them mates whom I knew needed the work. I felt like a thoroughly upstanding member of society, an all-round good guy. But all the time the pressure was building up inside my head, and the demons were swirling around.

One Boxing Day I was messing around with Angela and a couple of friends. I'd had some drinks and I was probably being a bit too boisterous.

'Stuart,' Angela's friend shouted, 'will you pack it in.'

I exploded, hurling the Christmas tree across the room
and screaming abuse at them, telling them I'd never liked
them and ordering them out of my house. 'You're an ani-
mal,' she said and left the room, leaving me feeling so sad
and sorry that I had allowed the demons to overpower
my self-control.

The only other time Angela had ever seen me lose it
quite like that was a few years before, when a bus driver
pulled out in front of us when we were in the car. At
the next set of lights I leapt out and ran to the front
of the bus, opened the emergency door and punched him.
I looked round and everyone in the bus was staring at me
in a stunned silence.

'Well, my wife's pregnant,' I said, with all the righteous indignation I could muster. 'And he just pulled out
in front of us.'

Angela was sitting quietly in the car when I got back.
'Stuart,' she said, 'I can't believe you've just done that.'

I was convinced that the driver had done it on purpose
and that he should have known Angela was pregnant. So
I was justified in protecting my wife and unborn child.
Mentally and physically I might have become a man, but
emotionally I was still a little boy, sure that I was justified in behaving the way I did because of what had happened to me in the past. Because I never talked to anyone
about what had happened, no one was able to explain to
me that I was wrong. I believed what I believed, and anyone who disagreed with me was out of order. Whenever
we had a row I would storm off like a child, swearing that

the relationship was over and that I didn't want to know her any more. If she upset me in any way I would just stop speaking to her. I had no coping mechanisms for any emotional situations.

In the midst of all this unhappiness, however, Angela told me she was pregnant again. She was pregnant just before Shirley died but had lost the baby. At the time she had accused me of not being bothered, but she was wrong. I was bothered and my way of dealing with it was to keep busy and keep working and distracted, when I should have been at home more, comforting and reassuring her. I did want another child, however, because having Matthew had been such a great experience.

Always being on the road, away from Angela and Matthew, added another layer of pressure. I started to doubt that Angela could possibly love me – how could she when I was such a naughty boy? She had never given me the slightest reason to doubt her, but still I did. The pressure built and built inside my head and one day I came home having made a decision. 'I don't want to be married any more,' I announced.

I can only imagine what a shock it was for Angela. She came from a very stable background with parents who had always stayed together and she had never thought for a moment that she would be any different. She cried when I told her and I stayed away for a few nights in Nottingham to give us both space to recover. I had never told her about my childhood, although I later discovered she had worked it out from the things I would shout out

in my sleep or when I was drunk, and she had no idea
that I didn't intend for us to stay together forever. Until
that moment I had no idea we weren't going to stay
together, either, but suddenly I knew I couldn't cope with
everything. Something had to give if I wasn't going to
lose my mind. Nothing Angela had ever done had merit-
ed such treatment. She was the perfect wife and the perfect mother; all the problems lay with me.

Angela gave birth to our daughter, Rebecca. Here was
another tiny, innocent person for me to care for and
guard from all the evils of the world. But I hadn't been
able to do anything to protect my friend Mark, or
Shirley, so what hope did I have of protecting my own
children? I really wanted to be there for the birth, as I
had been for Matthew's, but I felt I didn't deserve to be.
Because of the way I had treated Angela I had shown I
was a naughty boy after all. I couldn't bear the idea of
what her parents must think of me and I chickened out
of facing them.

All I could see was that I had to keep on working
every hour that I wasn't asleep, keeping myself distracted, proving that I was a good boy. I was unable to spend
even a few hours on my own for fear of what thoughts
would rise up and haunt me. I was even willing to sacri-
fice the bond I had with Matthew, and the one I wanted
to build with Rebecca, if it meant I could escape my own
thoughts and memories. It was madness but it took me
six months to realize what a mistake I'd made, and by
that time the damage was irreparable. I had pushed

Angela too far and there was no way she was going to take me back.

I fell out with my partners at work and left the company, leaving myself with endless time to think about everything that was wrong with my life and what a terrible person I was. Unable to exist on my own I started going out with other girls, and Angela found out. She was so angry she started making it difficult for me to see the children. I now had no work and no home, no marriage and no access to my kids. I was back with Mum. Knowing that I had let everybody down, I felt like I had nothing left to live for and killing myself began to seem like a good idea.

I went down to the railway and stood beside the line waiting for a train to come, ready to throw myself under the wheels. But when it came to it I couldn't do it. The train roared on by and I felt I had failed yet again. I went home and tried again to end it with a bottle of paracetamols. When Mum couldn't get any response from me she phoned an ambulance. I spent three days in hospital, during which I got to see a psychiatrist who suggested I go into counselling. I thought it would be a good idea and he said he would put my name on the waiting list. 'We'll call you,' he said. But they never did. It was a moment when I might have been able to let it all out, but once I was back home again the mental wounds scabbed over once more and everything was shut in as it always had been.

Every day seemed the same. I would wake up, throw open the curtains every morning and life would still be shit. I slashed my wrists, to show how much I hated myself, the same day I was due to go to court to try to get some sort of structured access to my children. The judge told me I wasn't mature enough to be responsible for small children. I felt like they were branding me as being like my dad, as being like all the paedophiles I had come across and read about in the papers. As I listened to his words I could feel the blood dripping down inside my sleeves from the wounds I had inflicted on myself and I knew he was right. I wasn't mature enough to be put in charge of my children; I was still a very naughty boy.

It was as if I was drifting away from the real world, with no one there to act as my anchor – no Shirley, no Angela, no Matthew. Mum and Christina were there, but they were as damaged as I was. I couldn't tell anyone what was going on in my head, so I was left alone with my horrible thoughts.

Christina had had another baby, with more post-natal depression, and had also developed a need to be constantly cleaning her house. If you asked her about it she would say it was because Mum always kept such a dirty home and she never wanted to be like that. She and Seb finally separated, which was Christina's choice. I still thought Seb was an amazing guy and I respected the way he tried to comfort and support her. In the end she was just too damaged and scarred by her own past for the relationship to ever stand a chance. We were both too messed up to be able to handle relationships with anyone.

I had a few relationships with women, but I was so needy they never worked out. I was using them, like drugs, to try to change the way I felt, needing my girl-friends to be constantly telling me they loved me, constantly comforting me and telling me I was doing well. I would do anything to please them, but I had to have the praise in return. They never lasted long. During one relationship I became so distressed I got drunk, slashed my arms, swallowed tablets and ended up in the special unit of a hospital for three or four weeks. Although some people close to me had guessed at what might have happened in my past, I still hadn't talked to anyone about it properly. I was ready to talk then, but the doctor didn't agree. He thought I was ready to leave.

'Don't you realize,' I said, 'one day I could end up killing somebody.'

He didn't want to know. I expect he had more than enough cases to deal with as it was, and he didn't want to get involved with someone as needy as I seemed to be. He gave me some anti-depressants and sent me on my way. I was a time bomb, just waiting to go off.

Chapter Twelve

TRACEY

Somehow I kept going. Knowing that I had always managed to find some release in my work, I approached an old friend who ran a steeplejacking company and asked if he would be interested in having me set up a lightning protection operation for him. He was happy with the idea so I was back in business and able to distract myself for at least a part of each day. All the guys who had worked with me in my last two companies came with me and the operation was up and running from day one.

I started a new relationship with Louise, the daughter of the landlady in the pub where I had battered the guy, and I moved in with her. She had an eight-year-old son called Andrew whom I got on with well, playing football and all that father–son stuff. I was still searching for the perfect family unit, even though I'd had it before and messed it up.

Angela began to relent about me seeing Matthew on Sundays. I wasn't allowed to take him to my Mum's or to

Louise's or to any other members of the family, which made it hard to pass the time with him. Nothing was open on Sundays, so we would end up just sitting by the local duck pond in the rain with him asking what we were going to do next. Louise was very keen for us all to be a family and I could see her point, so eventually I took Matthew home. When Angela found out she was furious and after that Matthew didn't want to come out with me at all. Angela still wasn't willing to allow me to take Rebecca out, although she would sometimes let me into the house to play with her for an hour or two. Angela was such a good mother to the kids I never wanted to argue or fight with her, I just hoped eventually she would relent. I wanted to share in their lives.

Things weren't going as well as I'd hoped at work, so I left and joined the local electricity company, Norweb, as a health and safety sales engineer. It was a really good job and I felt proud of myself, despite feelings of being rejected by my previous employer.

A friend of mine moved in with Angela, which I was perfectly OK with, but he didn't like me coming round to the door and talking to the kids. The situation went from bad to worse until one day when I turned up to see the kids the police were called to escort me away from the door. A few days later I received a solicitor's letter telling me that in future I was to draw up outside the house in the car when I came to take Matthew out and beep the horn once. It made me feel like I was a paedophile or some other sort of criminal who couldn't be trusted around children in the normal way. It made me feel like my dad. Determined to fight my corner, I went to court to try to get proper access. In the end I was told that Matthew had been interviewed and he didn't want me to take him out any more because of an incident when I pushed a man who had walked into him, and another when I shouted at someone from the car. I had no idea either of these incidents had had any effect on him at all. I was left feeling like some horrible man who didn't know how to treat kids. Yet again, it seemed, I had been a naughty boy.

Angela then read out a statement in court saying that she knew I had been physically abused and tortured as a child, and that she thought I had been sexually abused as well. I couldn't believe she was saying these things out loud in front of other people and in a fury I stormed out of the court. I drove out into the country, feeling completely despairing, parked up and slashed my wrists. A friend's girlfriend found me and took me to the hospital to be stitched up yet again. They always wanted to freeze my arms when they stitched me but I would never allow them; I thought I deserved to suffer. Sometimes they used staples and they really hurt. Yet again the doctors promised they would contact me about my seeing a psychiatrist and yet again nothing happened.

By the time I went back to work it was high summer, but I had to wear long sleeves all the time to cover up the growing patchwork of scars I had given myself. My relationship with Louise ended and I found someone else, still searching for the fairy-tale ending, still making all the same mistakes. It ended up with me getting drunk on whisky and slashing myself with a carving knife. The police were called and I was admitted to the psychiatric hospital.

I met a girl working in there, Lorraine, whom I had known a little before. I told her I had been abused and that was at the root of all my problems.

'I know,' she said.

'How do you know?' I was startled.

'You told me, a long time ago, after you'd had a few drinks. I told you then you needed to talk to someone. You wanted to talk to me but I wasn't really the right person, and I knew you as a friend so I couldn't really do it.'

But all they did was drug me up to calm me down enough to discharge me. There was a shortage of beds and they wanted to move me on. I was sat in front of a panel of experts who pontificated a lot and then basically told me I had to leave the hospital. 'Can't you see the way my life's going?' I pleaded. 'I could end up killing someone.'

I was now being permanently haunted by flashbacks and nightmares, as if someone had broken open every box that I had so carefully locked away at the back of my mind. Now the memories were out it was impossible to get them back into the boxes. The occupational health people at work sent me to be assessed and I thought maybe they would get me some counselling, but all they said was that I was fit to go back to work. I slunk back feeling humiliated, certain that everyone now knew all about my past and my life.

I split up with my girlfriend and didn't know where to go. Mum had settled in permanently with Trevor by then and I knew they didn't want me back. I didn't feel I was wanted anywhere. I didn't like living on my own – it gave me too much time to think. I soon started another relationship and I also met up with someone I hadn't seen for a long time. When I'd known him before he had been a puny little fellow and I was shocked to see that he had developed into a really strong, muscular-looking man.

'What happened to you?' I asked when we got talking.

'I've been going to the gym,' he said.

'I've been thinking of trying that.'

'Why don't you come with me,' he suggested.

Even though I was a big man, and strong enough to win virtually all the fights I got myself into, I always felt vulnerable and weak because of what had happened to me. Within weeks of going to the gym I was hooked on making myself as big and muscular as I possibly could. I wanted it to be obvious to anyone who looked at me that I wasn't to be messed with. I wanted to be invincible and invulnerable. I wanted to be free of all fear. I started working out five or six times a week and my friend worked me out a diet. He also suggested I take some steroids to hasten the process up. I agreed and let him inject me in the backside. There weren't many people I would have trusted to do something so personal for me, but I had complete faith in him, having known him since he was a kid. He was one of the funniest guys I'd ever met, always able to make me laugh uncontrollably. He still did mad things, like shoplifting manikins and other eccentric items, and he allowed me to be a kid again in a stupid, funny way.

Getting hold of steroids in gyms is never a problem; the problem is the side effects. Because they increase the testosterone in your system they tend to make you more angry and aggressive. Men who body build tend to want to show their bodies off, so they go to clubs, where all the other drugs are readily available as well, and get into the world of doormen and bouncers. That inevitably leads to the shadowy world of gangsters, and the pretty girls who hang around with them because they want to be part of something exciting and glamorous. I followed exactly this path and within no time I was snorting cocaine, amazed by how great I felt, my fears gone and my mood elevated. It even made me less fearful about sex; it seemed to be the answer to all my problems.

The trouble was, when the effects of the coke wore off, I was back in my old depressing world. I was putting all my efforts into trying to find a place in life where I fitted in, but as soon as I sobered up I was left asking the same old question – why me? Why did all that bad stuff have to happen to me? Was I really that naughty?

People were starting to notice that I was getting muscular and I felt good about myself physically. I began wearing shorts and T-shirts. I was hanging out with other body-building guys at weekends. I felt like I was 'somebody' at last. I got to know all the doormen at the clubs, doing a bit of door work myself. It felt great to be able to walk to the front of queues outside pubs and clubs and have the barrier lifted for me by someone who recognized me. I had a smart BMW from work. I was starting to look as if I was amounting to something. When I was feeling good I could tell myself I could forget about my dysfunctional family and my broken marriage. I found myself talking to some of the big guys from the tough areas, fitting in, getting respect. This, I decided, was what I had been missing all those years; this was where I was meant to be. On weekdays, I was still working at Norweb and no one there had any idea what I was involved with in the evenings and at weekends.

Looking back of course I can see that we were all taking steroids because we were full of fear, and we were all snorting coke in an effort to change the way that we felt. We all stuck together because like-minded people attract and we all wanted the same things, probably for very similar reasons. There are a lot of damaged people out there.

I started a relationship with Lorraine from the hospital, who worked as a play specialist for sick children. Her family were very warm and welcoming, but I had trouble believing I was really part of it. They were such a lovely family and I desperately wanted a family of my own. I still had all the same problems with insecurity and jealousy and I took more and more coke to keep my confidence up, to give me the buzz I needed. I'd taken to gambling as well, because it provided yet another way to change the way I felt in the short term. I started to get into debt on my credit card. Eventually I drove Lorraine and me apart. I always left people first because I was afraid they would leave me and I didn't know how I would handle it. Lorraine never did anything wrong, any more than Angela did, and there was nothing wrong with the relationship, beyond the fact that I was sick.

Mum had moved out of Platting Grove by this time and ran her own pub up in Oldham, although I still had keys to the place and Mum often asked me to check the house to make sure everything was OK. I sometimes used to go there to cry or to be alone. Whenever I wasn't distracting myself and altering my mood by artificial means like drink, drugs, body-building or gambling, my depression was growing worse. I wanted somebody to look after me, to put their arms around me and tell me everything was going to be OK, but if anyone had tried I would probably have pushed them away. There seemed no point in going on, so I parked my car in the garage at Platting Grove, shut the door, fed a hosepipe from the exhaust in through the window and settled down with pictures of Shirley and my kids. I turned on the engine and waited to die. Within a few minutes I was asleep.

I was shocked to wake up the next morning and find I was still alive. The engine was still running but the hosepipe had fallen out of the window. I switched the engine off and climbed groggily out of the car. Opening the garage door I was dazzled by the sunlight outside. It was a beautiful warm day and I was still there to enjoy it. I actually felt happy to be alive. I wondered if Shirley was trying to tell me something; maybe it just wasn't time for me to go yet. I even wondered if perhaps I was dead and this was what it felt like.

I made up with Lorraine and tried once more to get on with my life. We went up to Scotland for the New Year's celebrations with a couple of friends, but I drank too much and the rage that was always suppressed below the surface, never allowed to escape, never resolved, exploded uncontrollably. I ended up smashing our hotel room to pieces in a miserable, furious rampage. It was getting harder and harder to control the demons in my head. Once I finished with the destruction I stormed through into the shower, picked up a razor and started slashing my hands, spraying blood around the room. We were about eight floors up and I tried to climb out of the window. Eventually I was calmed down and taken, shaking with emotion, to Edinburgh Royal Infirmary. All I remember of the next few hours was hearing them saying they were going to have to staple me up. I have no idea what had caused me to lose it so badly.

When I got home my doctor finally managed to get me in to see a counsellor, but I knew immediately from the questions she was asking that the woman had no idea how to deal with someone with my background. I got more comfort from the coke I was snorting in larger and larger quantities, the fruit machines and the Jack Daniels bottle. I kept taking the steroids because I liked the way I was looking. I started using sun beds to give myself a tan and visited a tanning shop in Ashton, where I met Tracey, a tiny, beautiful girl who was working on reception. I couldn't get her out of my mind, which made me wonder if I really did love Lorraine. The other girls in the shop told me that their colleague liked me, which made me feel good. They told me she went to a club which was one of my regular haunts as well – in fact I was one of the people controlling the drugs and what went on there.

The next weekend she was there, and just as beautiful as I remembered. I started talking to her friends, not wanting to make a direct hit on her, so she started dancing with my mate, which worried me, but by the end of the evening I had got chatting with her. I found out she was in a relationship with a guy she didn't love and wasn't happy. I told her I was in the same position. From that moment on we started seeing one another.

A lot of my friends liked to take ecstasy when out dancing and I became curious. My body-building mate was always going on about how good it was, but I'd never got up the nerve to use it, having heard that it could kill you. I decided that if he did it, it must be OK, so I took one tab and it was fantastic. My confidence rose five hundred per cent and I even wanted to dance, something I never usually did. My legs and arms just started to move, able to get a rhythm they had never got before. It was even better than drinking and snorting coke. We started travelling to clubs in Leeds and Sheffield and Manchester every weekend, from Friday to Sunday.

The weeks, however, were another matter, the comedown dragging my spirits back into depression and leaving me shaking, shivering, sweating and crying uncontrollably. I continually questioned why Shirley had to die, why I didn't have a proper dad, why Dad had done the things he'd done. The nightmares and flashbacks that I could drive away during the weekends with drugs and dancing were unstoppable when I was sober.

I moved in with Tracey and her two teenage kids. She was brilliant at dealing with my moods and jealousies. The drugs were the most important thing to me and I would often finish with her on a Friday and disappear off into clubland for two days, where I felt important and part of the scene, where everyone was friendly and no one ever judged or criticized me, only to crawl back and ask for forgiveness on the Monday. She was endlessly patient and understanding.

Part of me really wanted to clean up my act and concentrate on my relationship with Tracey. I went back to the doctor and told her I thought I was in real trouble in my head and she booked me in to see a psychiatrist and gave me some anti-depressants. The session with the psychiatrist went well; he could see there was a dark side to my life that needed addressing and I felt optimistic about the future. I asked Tracey if she wanted to go away to Blackpool for the weekend, thinking we could do some drugs and dance and have a good time.

'No,' she said, 'I'd rather go somewhere quiet, just the two of us.'

'What about Wales then?' I asked, not really thinking about it, but knowing it was quiet and relaxing.

'OK.'

Trevor lent us his camper van and we set off, holding hands, listening to music, feeling very in love, like we were making a fresh start. We found a campsite but the van wasn't really that comfortable, so we changed our minds and decided to look for a guesthouse. We booked into a place called The Rose Tor and got given a lovely room. I was determined I was going to turn my life around from now on, stop knocking around with the door lads all the time, and cut down on the drink and drugs. After a lovely meal we went to bed.

'If the weather's nice we'll go for a walk tomorrow up the hills,' I suggested, feeling really happy.

The next morning the weather had turned a bit chilly, and Tracey wasn't feeling too well, so we decided to scrap the walk. We wandered around the shops of Llandudno instead, not wanting the day to end, feeling romantic.

'Would you like to see where I used to stay when I was a kid?' I asked.

We drove out into the countryside and reached the area where my Auntie Doris lived. The little Victorian houses dotting the roads looked so familiar and memories started to surface, many of them happy memories of things I used to do with my cousin John. There was a café, which had a submarine game we used to play, and then we passed the Spa shop.

'That's where I stayed with my dad when he had a flat over the shop,' I said. A picture of the young prostitute came into my mind. A mile further on down the road we turned right down a hill and came to a row of cottages that included my Auntie Doris's. It had changed a bit, but not so much that I wouldn't have known where I was. I could see the railway where John and I used to play, and the quarry where we had climbed on the hoppers. They were good memories. I pulled up on a little bridge and stared at the house for a moment. I could even see their old outside toilet. I remembered how frightened I was to go out there in the dark, surrounded with spiders.

'That's where I nearly hung John, once,' I said, looking down at the mossy bridge. 'We were being James Bond. I was lowering him on a rope, having tied it round his shoulders and neck, and it nearly killed him. My uncle had to come out and rescue him.'

'You all right?' Tracey asked.

'Yeah. I had some good times here. I really loved my cousins. John was probably the only real friend I had as a child.'

After a few minutes I drove back up the hill to the main road and suddenly saw my uncle Stuart, standing beside a parked car. He stared straight at me and my heart skipped a beat. I'd always liked him, but he was still a reminder of my past. I stopped the van.

'You all right, pal?' he said, coming over. 'You lost?'

'You all right, Uncle Stuart?'

'Bleedin' hell, it's Stuart. Look at the size of you!' Before I could say a word he'd turned and shouted back towards the car. 'Doris, it's Stu! Come in, lad, come in.' Before I could protest we were being swept into the house. My heart was thumping. I was suddenly petrified but I knew I couldn't just drive off. Doris was as stone-faced as ever.

It was all so confusing. They were offering us tea and the television was going, with news of a child's abduction and murder and a Russian submarine trapped at the bottom of the ocean and so many images were flashing through my mind at once I couldn't focus on anything.

'Let me phone John and let him know you're here,' Stuart was saying. 'He'll be really pleased to see you. You were close as kids, you two.'

'Does our David know you're here?' Doris piped in. 'Do you want us to go and get him? I'll send Lee over to get him...' Lee was my youngest cousin.

I wanted to burst into tears; everything was happening at once, going too fast for me to control. I certainly wasn't ready to face my father after all this time. All my emotions were rising up like a tidal wave and I wanted to run out of the house before I was washed away. John turned up with his girlfriend, Angeline, and there was another round of introductions and more reminiscences.

'That your Range Rover outside?' I asked him.

'No, it's your dad's, he's lent it to me. Does he know you're here?'

'We need to get back,' I lied, panicked by the casual way they all talked about Dad, as if it would be the most natural thing in the world for me to see him after all this time. 'We've got friends waiting for us in Llandudno. Tell him I'll be in touch.'

I just wanted to get out. Doris was starting to talk about Dad's second wife, Barbara, in the same derogatory terms she had always talked about Mum, claiming she was just after Dad's money, just using him. I wasn't interested in hearing whatever it was she had to say and blocked it out. Once we were safely in the car and driving away from the noise and the people my childhood memories came sweeping back over me in all their gory detail.

'They haven't got a clue, have they?' I said out loud, unable to stop the tears from coming. 'They haven't got a clue how devastated our family was by what he did.'

I was driving at a snail's pace, the traffic building up behind me. I'd told Tracey more about my past than anyone else and she understood what I was going through. I wound through some country roads, without knowing where I was going, and pulled over, completely lost. I was feeling sick with depression and needed to clear my head. We got out and walked up some hills, holding hands. She put her arm around me to comfort me. I wanted her to know that I wasn't going to let this affect me or change my mind about our new start together. I wanted to show that my dad couldn't still be affecting my life after so many years. But of course he was. I'd tried using drink, drugs, sex, the gym, working, starting a family, and nothing would clean him out of my mind. I needed her to take away the pain, to soothe me, but her gentleness aroused me, and my arousal brought back flashes of memory from the past, making me feel dirty and angry with myself for behaving like Dad.

'I don't want to go back home,' I said when we got back to the van. 'Can't we just drive somewhere else?'

'I can't, Stuart,' she protested. 'I've got work tomorrow.'

'Can we do something tonight, because I just want to forget this.'

'OK.'

I drove Tracey home, promising to come back for her later to take her for a drink. Her son had filled the house with his friends and I didn't fancy going in. I drove the van back to Trevor, with Dad on my mind all the time. I wondered if he knew that I had done well with my work, that he had grandkids. I wanted him to know that I was a good boy now, not a naughty one. I wondered if he still had any feelings for me, any love. I felt the same urge to see him and ask him the questions that were spinning round in my head as I had when I was fourteen. Nothing had really changed in nearly twenty years.

Chapter Thirteen

THE LUMP HAMMER

I saw Mum as I went into the pub.

'You all right, chuck?'

'Yeah,' I said, my voice subdued. 'I went to Wales today. I saw Stuart and Doris. They've no idea, have they? Dad's just carrying on with another life down there as if nothing ever happened.'

I could see she didn't have time to stop and chat, busy getting ready to go out. It was always the same. If I ever tried to ask her questions about Dad and about our childhood she would brush me aside with 'the past is the past'.

I went to my room and sat down on the bed with my head spinning round. I must have fallen asleep and when I woke I felt the lead weight of depression, like my head was being squeezed in a vice. I went for a shower, feeling dirty, my childhood still running past me like a horror movie on a constant loop, never stopping. I kept coming back to all the questions I wanted to ask Dad, the ones he had always avoided answering in the past. Did he miss me? Did he still love me? Had he changed? Did he want me back in his life? Why did he do what he did? Had he thought about the damage he had done?

I got dressed and went down to the car to go and pick Tracey up. The next thing I knew I was back on the motorway to Wales, having switched my phone off so I didn't have to explain any more to Tracey. I knew she thought I was lying, that I was going back on my promise to make a new start and that I was just going off to the clubs to try to drown all the demons that the trip to Wales had unleashed, but it was beyond my ability to convince her otherwise at that moment. I wasn't in a fit state to explain anything to anyone. I couldn't work out what was going on in my own mind anyway.

When I got to Wales I stopped and turned the phone back on again. I dialled Doris's number. Uncle Stuart answered.

'Hi,' I said, 'it's Stuart. Have you got Dad's address?'

'Why? Are you going to write to him?'

'Yeah.'

I didn't want to tell him I planned to go and visit Dad because I didn't want all of them turning up as well. I wanted to talk to him alone. You can't talk about personal things when other people are there, especially the sort of things I wanted to talk about. Stuart gave me the address.

'Thanks. Have you got the phone number?'

'Hang on,' he said. 'Doris knows that.'

Doris came on the line and gave me a number. I thanked her and hung up. I rang the number but it didn't connect to anything. A few minutes later, she rang me back. 'Hi, Stuart,' she said. 'I think I may have given you the wrong number before.' Doris seemed a little suspicious of me that day and must have been curious. Dad may even have told her about our past, given that he was closer to her than anyone. She said in her statement later that she called my dad for permission to give his number to me.

She gave me the right number. I rang it, but still couldn't get an answer. Pulling back out on to the road I started driving around, having no idea where the address Uncle Stuart had given me might be. I was becoming increasingly nervous the closer I got. My body was shaking with fear, just as it had done when I was a small boy preparing myself to go in through the back door and face a battering. I was trying to picture how I would break the ice when I found the house. How would I start the conversation? I decided to buy a couple of beers. That would be a good way to start, to make it seem more like a normal visit. I pulled up outside the Spa shop and went in. I picked up a couple of bottles and walked to the till, shocked to find John's girlfriend Angeline on the till.

'Hi, Stuart,' she said. 'I thought you went home.'

'Yeah, I've come back.'

'Have you come to see your dad?'

'Yeah, I thought I'd pop up to see him.'

'Does he know you're coming?'

'No.'

'Well, he was out before, but he should be back in by now.'

I thanked her, paid for the beer and left without thinking to ask where his house was. I drove round a few more roads and just as I was about to give up and go home, I saw the green Range Rover Discovery John had been driving that morning. Assuming he had given it back to Dad by now, I parked the BMW and got out, so shaky and breathless that I forgot all about the bottles of beer.

The house was a little way from the parking space, through a gap in a stone wall and up a track. As I walked towards it I saw the back garden, laid out exactly like our back garden had been in Cranbrook Street. I was about to go to the back door, as I had been trained to do, then remembered I was an adult, visiting another adult. It would be all right for me to go to the front. I walked round to the other side of the house, which looked out towards the sea. It was like walking back in time to our old home. I got to a gate and saw two silver dog bowls standing outside the door and stopped dead in my tracks. A vision of myself crouched down, eating from them while Dad masturbated, came into my head. If the dog bowls were here, I realized that the other side of the house must be the front.

I was confused now to be approaching what felt like the wrong side of the house, terrified of what I was going to find. As I went through the gate I noticed there was a film flickering through the crack in some drawn curtains in what must be the front room and my heart beat increased as I remembered all those terrible times when he used to show us films. I was so filled with fear I could hardly breathe, but I knew I couldn't turn back now. I wanted us to be able to talk, for him to explain things to me and for us to become friends.

There was a bell by the glass door, just like at Cranbrook Street, and my hand hovered above it for what seemed like hours. A movement behind the curtains made me think he'd spotted me and I pressed the button quickly. There was no going back now. As the inside door opened his face appeared. He'd aged a bit, but he still looked the same. There was grey in his hair, making it look like he'd had it streaked. And he had the same twisted look round his mouth that I'd seen a thousand times before when he was beating or abusing me.

'Who is it?' he asked.

'It's Stuart. Don't you remember me, Dad?'

Although he was over six feet tall, I was a good three inches taller than him now, and much stronger looking, but I still felt like a frightened little boy as he turned round and walked back into the house without a word, leaving the door open for me to follow. He went straight back into the sitting room and sat down on the settee again. I could tell it must have been where he was sitting before because there was the bowl of water on the floor and he had his shoes and socks off. Pictures of all the times he made me wash his feet in an identical bowl came rushing back. I could remember the vile smell and how dirty it used to make me feel to have to touch them.

The whole room was laid out exactly like Cranbrook Street. There was a collection of brand new toy cars on display and I remembered how we never got any new toys when we were children.

'You all right?' I asked, still standing over him, twisting my body uncomfortably, still not able to look him in the eyes, even though I was now a grown man, casting them down to the floor in an agony of fear. That was the rule; to look at him directly could get me a beating. He didn't bother to reply.

'I need to ask you what ... I don't understand ...' The words were falling over one another in my panic to get them out and my fear of how he would react. 'Why did you hurt us?' I started to cry.

'I never,' he snapped, as if he was already fed up with my accusations, as if he'd heard them a hundred times before and was bored with the whole subject.

'I wasn't naughty, Dad.'

I couldn't stop shaking and tried to disguise it by sitting down, crouching like I used to as a child. I didn't want him to know how frightened I was, but I couldn't think how to act more naturally either. The foot bowl was in just the same position it had always been, and so was his ashtray. He was sitting in exactly the same position he always sat in when he kept the belt or brass fork to hand to beat me. He started shouting at me and I was unable to stop the sobs, transported back in time a quarter of a century, as terrified as I had always been.

He just kept on shouting at me, ranting and denying everything, furious that I dared to question him and accuse him. He leant forward and I saw the lump hammer, like a small sledge hammer, the sort that builders and steeplejacks use, on the settee beside him, in just the same place he would have kept the belt or the fork or a walking stick, or whatever other weapon he wanted to try out on me. He must have been expecting me. He was ready and waiting to punish me in the same way he always had. Or maybe he'd been warned I was on my way and that I was a big, dangerous-looking guy now and he felt he needed to defend himself. I didn't have time to think it through; I just knew I had to get the hammer before he used it on me. I lunged across behind him and grabbed it. He was standing up to attack me, I was certain. I'd seen that look on his face so many times and I knew what it meant. I was about to get a battering and God knows what else. I lashed out at his head, desperate to stop him.

'Please, Daddy, no!'

I dropped the hammer and ran from the house without looking back, terrified he would be behind me, that he would grab me and pull me back inside to punish me for daring to hit back. As I ran down the hill I was sure I could feel his presence behind me, as I had done so many times before. I reached the car and tore open the door, started the engine and roared away, still not daring to look back. I saw the bottles of beer and hurled them out the window, without knowing why. Not knowing what to do, I dialled everyone I could think of.

'Tracey, help me, something terrible's happened. I don't know what I've done. Please meet me at the pub.'

'Christina, you know I love you, don't you? Please meet me at the pub.'

'Seb, I don't know what I've done. I think I've hurt him.'

'Mum, please can you and Trevor come back to the pub straight away, something really serious has happened and I need to speak to you.'

I rang one friend after another as I drove at full speed, trying to escape from my past. I was so terrified I wanted everyone to be there and to protect me from the demons. I didn't know if I had really hurt him, but I knew I would have angered him and he would want to punish me. He would be coming after me because I had done something really naughty. I was shaking with the shock, driving as fast as the BMW would allow me, desperate to get to the safety and security of my friends and family before Dad caught up with me. I just wanted people to hold me and tell me everything was going to be OK. I wanted everyone I cared for to be together, frightened that he might come after them as well as me. We needed to be able to defend ourselves. My head was completely scrambled.

When I pulled into the pub car park Tracey was already there, looking frightened and concerned. I jumped out of the car and ran to her.

'Tracey, I don't know what I've done. I've hit him with a hammer.'

'What do you mean? What are you on about?'

At that moment Christina turned up and they hustled me inside the pub and upstairs, away from prying eyes as I tried to stutter out the story. Other people arrived and I could see they were all looking at me in a funny way. The more I tried to straighten the story out in my mind, the more I babbled nonsensically.

'Have you been taking drugs Stuart?' someone asked.

'What do you mean?'

'Are you sure you've been to Wales tonight? You seem very calm if all this has just happened.'

Calm? How could they think I was calm? I was shaking and hardly able to get my words out. It was starting to sink in that I had hit Dad with a hammer; the chances that he was still chasing me were slight, but the chances I had done him a serious injury were high. As my memory began to settle down the gravity of what might have happened started to sink in. For the first time ever I told them that Dad had sexually abused me too, just like he had Christina and Shirley, and God alone knew how many other people we knew nothing about. It was obvious from their faces that they were stunned. They'd all seen how he had bullied and beaten me, but it had never occurred to them what else he was doing when he came up to my bedroom, ordering Christina to wait downstairs until he came back. They had assumed it was just more beatings. Mum and Trevor could see things were serious, even if they weren't sure quite what had happened yet. They went downstairs to clear the pub out for the night and then came back up.

'We need to call the police,' Mum said.

As I calmed down I felt a terrible weariness coming over me. I didn't think I could cope with what was going to happen now. I just wanted to kill myself and end the whole horrible thing once and for all. I looked round at Mum and Christina, Tracey and Clare, and I started to give them all hugs.

'I'm going out for an hour,' I said.

I walked outside and got into the car. I couldn't mess it up this time. I had to succeed. I took the car out on to the motorway and headed for a spot known as 'Death Valley', where I was confident I could drive myself off the road. I pulled over for a few minutes to compose myself, then drew out on to carriageway and accelerated the car up to its maximum. I wanted to end the pain and the misery once and for all, but when it came to turning the wheel and deliberately destroying myself I just couldn't do it. Yet again it seemed something was stopping me. I drove on down the motorway for a bit and then turned, determined to do it on the way back. I pressed the accelerator to the floor and felt the power of the engine building. The phone rang, making me start. I picked up.

'Stuart?' It was Tracey, and I could tell she was crying. 'Stuart, I love you more than anything in the world. Whatever you've been through we'll get through it. We all love you. Your mum's here and Christina and we all love you. We don't want anything to happen to you.'

At that moment I knew I was loved. I lifted my foot off the accelerator and the engine settled down again. I was crying now as well. They were all there when I got back to the pub and I felt overcome with exhaustion. It was like walking through a bad dream, not really knowing what was real and what was my imagination, having no idea what was going to happen next or what I should do.

'I've phoned the police, Stuart,' Mum said.

'Why?' I asked.

'Stuart, I had to. They want you to phone the station.'

All I wanted was to go to bed and sleep forever, but I made the call. I told them I thought I might have hurt my dad, but they said there had been no reports of any incidents but that they would get back to me if they heard anything. I suppose most of the calls they get turn out to be false alarms or situations that just sort themselves out. They certainly didn't make it seem like a big deal, which made the whole thing seem even more surreal and dream-like. I was pretty sure I'd done something very naughty and would deserve to be punished, but no one else seemed to be too bothered. I went to bed and Tracey hugged me and tried to reassure me that everything was going to be OK.

A few hours later I was woken by a phone call. I answered it, still groggy and confused, not sure if I had dreamed the whole thing. A policeman from Manchester introduced himself, confirmed that I was the right person and then informed me that they had police at the back and front entrances to the pub and asked me to come out quietly. My first worry was Tracey and then Clare.

'Listen,' I said, the memories of the previous day beginning to come together, 'I'm a big bloke, but I don't want any heavy stuff when I come out.'

'That's OK, lad,' he assured me. 'That won't happen.'

In fact the police were already inside the building. By the time I had pulled some clothes on they had arrived in the bedroom. They took me downstairs and there were more of them there. Everything had changed. They now knew what had happened in Wales and whereas a few hours before everyone, including me, had been wondering if I had imagined the whole thing, we all now knew it was real.

'Is he all right?' I asked. 'Is he all right?'

'We need to talk about that, lad,' the senior officer said.

He cautioned me and then told me he was arresting me on suspicion of murder. Gradually I learned what had happened. I had caved Dad's skull in with the hammer, but I hadn't killed him instantly. He had been brain dead by the time Doris and Stuart and the others were alerted that there was something wrong, but he had died from his injuries by the time he reached hospital. It must have been terrible for the family when they got to the house; there was a lot of blood and his brain was hanging out of his head. The local police quickly got the impression that a cold, calculating killer had driven down from Manchester in his black BMW to execute this well-loved family man and upstanding employee of the local council.

I asked if I could say good-bye to Tracey and the officer said yes. I was walking about in a trance, unable to believe that I had actually killed my own dad. Tracey was crying and my mind just went completely blank. As we came out into the fresh air I could see police vehicles all the way up and down the street, like they had come to arrest Al Capone. As they guided me into the back of one of the cars, I just kept saying, 'It's not my fault, it's not my fault,' like a child who's been accused of breaking something.

Chapter Fourteen

FORGET EVERYTHING

When we got to the police station they put me in a paper suit. Everyone seemed to be looking at me really nastily, as if I was some kind of killer monster and I suppose that was how it looked. There were people there from North Wales and they told me they were taking me down there, as that was where the crime had been committed. I didn't want to be taken that far away from Tracey and Mum and Christina.

The duty solicitor, Ash Halam, a nice young guy, came in to see me.

'You are on a very serious charge here,' he said.

'I know,' I replied, 'but I have to get to work in a minute.' I hated the idea of letting my bosses down and getting into trouble.

'Forget work,' he said. 'You can forget anything for a long time.'

'What do you mean?' I was still in shock. I couldn't work out what was going to happen next.

'They're going to take you to North Wales now and I'll come down to see you there. If any other solicitors ask you if you want representation, tell them no. We'll look after you.'

I guess he could already see that this was going to be a big case and he wanted to keep it for his firm. I've since heard that the average cost of defending a murder charge is a million pounds, so I represented a lot of potential income for his firm. I nodded dumbly. I liked him and just wanted him to sort everything out for me, so I could go back to work and back to Tracey.

Once we got to Wales they brought me a pie and chips, but I couldn't swallow, I was too tense and frightened. It reminded me of how hard it was to eat whenever Dad was threatening me or hitting me. I just kept rambling on to anyone who was around: 'I'm sorry about this. It wasn't my fault. I was abused as a kid.'

Ash arrived after a few hours and I asked if I could see Tracey. I felt so alone and vulnerable and confused.

'No, you can't see her,' he said. 'She's part of the investigation. They're going to interview you now and you are not to say anything, leave everything to me. I believe you are mentally unstable, but you mustn't say anything at this stage. I'm here to protect you and serve you. You are being charged with murder, and you could end up being put in prison for twenty-five years. So let me do my job. If you answer one question they will know you are capable of answering others. So even if they ask you if you want a drink of water, don't answer beyond giving your name and address. Everything else is "no comment".'

I just stared at him in a daze. I was willing to do whatever he told me but it didn't feel honest somehow. All through the interview I wanted to answer the police questions honestly, but each time I had to say, 'no comment'. It continued to feel like a terrible dream and I wanted to wake up. They questioned me for more than forty-eight hours before they charged me with murder. I pleaded not guilty.

The next morning I was handcuffed and then double cuffed to a security man who took me out to a police van, known as a 'sweatbox', where prisoners are separated into minute cubicles to be transported about. Ever since being locked in the cellar as a child I'd had real problems with confined spaces. Inside the van my knees were pressed up against the wall so I couldn't move an inch, and the sweat started to pour from every inch of my skin.

They put the radio on and drove me about a hundred yards from the police station to the courtroom. There were other people waiting in the cells and I felt full of fear as I was directed in, a familiar feeling of being at the centre of a buzzing electrical storm, all my senses heightened and poised for flight but unable to go anywhere.

Ash, the solicitor, was in court with me and when the magistrates retired after hearing an outline of the case I asked him if I would be able to get bail.

'No, Stuart,' he said, sadly. 'You won't be getting bail.'

'Why not?'

'Because of the seriousness of the offence. I'll apply for it, but we won't get it. You'll be sent straight to remand prison.'

'But I want to go home. I want to see my mum and Tracey.'

It still hadn't occurred to me that I wouldn't be going home. I hadn't imagined I would be going to prison. I had no bag and no clothes apart from a few things a friend had brought in for me. I didn't understand how my life could have changed so suddenly and completely. The magistrates came back and I thought their spokeswoman looked a bit tearful when she told me I was going into custody. I still didn't really understand what she was talking about. The security officer told me to come with him.

'Where am I going, Ash?' I asked, panic-stricken. 'Are you coming with me?'

'No, Stuart, I can't come with you.'

'Well, who's going to come with me? Will I not be seeing my mum and Tracey?'

The guard took me to a cell and I sat down and cried, begging for help from God or Shirley or anyone else who might be listening. If I'd had the means to kill myself at that moment I probably would have tried again. The sweatbox that came to pick me up picked up other men as well. I was frightened to think I was going to be amongst real criminals, which wasn't how I saw myself. I was just a naughty boy. This was exactly the fate that Dad had threatened me with if I ever told anyone about how bad I was and how he had to punish me.

No doubt if the other men in the van had known why I was there they would have been even more afraid of me than I was of them, particularly with my size and the physique I had built for myself in the gym. I'd wanted to make myself look intimidating in order to be invulnerable, but my appearance now made me seem a threat to others, making me even more vulnerable.

Through the tiny slit of a window in the side of the van I could see we were being driven through some big high gates. It looked like the entrance to a sports stadium. It still didn't occur to me that I was on my way to Altcourse prison in Liverpool. As they unlocked the doors of the van a guy in the next cubicle was singing. He seemed off his head and I felt a new tremor of fear as my sweat cooled in the fresh air.

We were taken through to a room. Our handcuffs were unlocked and we were stood in line. The other guys all seemed to know what they were meant to do.

'Next.'

It was my turn.

'Name.'

I gave it.

'Open your mouth.'

'What?'

'Open your mouth!' the guard shouted.

I obeyed and he peered inside, inspecting my tongue, making me feel violated like I used to when Dad forced himself into my mouth.

'Take your shoes off.'

I obeyed, stepping out of them and leaving them on the floor.

'Do you think I'm fucking picking them up?'

'Sorry?'

'You heard me. Pick your fucking shoes up!'

He searched my trainers and then sent me through to the next room where all the other lads were talking as if they already knew one another. Some doors slid open and we went through into a kind of holding pen. Through a wall of bars we could see the prisoners already inside below us, at home in that hostile, frightening place. I saw a group of lads eyeing us up and down and felt a warning prickle of fear. One of them sauntered up towards me and spoke to another guy close by.

'You're a fucking beast, you. I know all about you.'

One of the guys in our group went up the bars and started shouting abuse at someone on the other side. The sounds of anger and raised voices stirred hundreds of fearful memories deep inside my head. I could see that I was going to have to fight my corner in this place. There was no way I was going to be allowed a quiet life unless I managed to win their respect.

They brought us some cold food and it tasted like shit. I couldn't swallow it and one of the other lads took it off me. He didn't seem to have any difficulty eating. As they led us further into the building, through turnstiles operated by key cards, past stacks of cells lowering over us like blocks of flats, I felt assaulted by the shouting and noise coming from every direction. Everywhere I looked

I could see rows of cells with people poking their heads round the doors to see what was going on. Finally the reality hit me. I was in prison. They gave us pillowcases with our 'plastics' in, which meant a plastic cup, plate, bowl and cutlery, plus a blanket, sheet and pillow.

A warder told me I was up on the second floor, pointing to my cell. As I walked towards it a hand flashed out of another cell and a Scouse accent said, 'Come in here.'

'Am I allowed to?'

''Course you are.' He pulled me into the cell with him. 'Fucking hell, you're a big lad, aren't you?'

'Yeah.' I grinned sheepishly.

'It would take a few of us to get you fucking down and get your trainers off you, wouldn't it?'

'Yeah it would,' I agreed. 'And I'd get every fucking one of you back.'

He started laughing, as if I'd passed some sort of test. 'Have you got any gear?' he asked.

'No,' I said.

'Do you want some?'

'I don't know.' I didn't want to offend him, but I didn't want to do anything wrong and get into trouble with the wardens either.

'I've got some weed here. Don't worry about the fucking screws, they won't come in here.' I made my excuses and went to my cell.

Later I was called back down by the wardens and asked if I wanted cigarettes. I took what they gave me, having no idea they were meant to last me a week.

Nothing was ever explained; you were expected to just pick things up as you went along. Next came a visit to the doctor.

'Do you have any problems?'

'Yes, I was abused when I was a kid and I'm frightened of being in cells with other people. I don't like having men around me. What am I going to do about taking showers and going to the toilet?'

'Are you on any medication?'

'Yeah, I'm on anti-depressants.'

'I'll put you down as depressive and try to get someone to come and talk to you, but I don't know how long that will be. That's all. Thank you.'

Everything was always a direct order, and they were always using our surnames, not our first names. It was intimidating. It was like being a child again, being shouted at, told what to do, locked up in dirty, confined places.

Back on the wing it was the same confusing mêlée.

'Right, lads,' came the orders, 'get your water and into your cells.'

They all started filling flasks with hot water, although I had no idea why. I made my way towards my allotted cell and someone intercepted me.

'Not going in there, are you?'

'Why not?'

'He's a dirty, scruffy bastard, full of crabs. You don't want to share with him.'

I peered into my cell and saw there was someone in there exactly fitting my informant's description. I felt a surge of panic. I couldn't share a cell. No way would I be able to deal with that.

'I'm not going in there,' I told a warden.

'Come downstairs then,' he said. 'I'll put you in with another lad.'

'No. You don't understand. I need a room on my own.'

'Can't do that.'

He led me to a cell with a lad from Macclesfield already on the top bunk. Everything about it was filthy. We chatted for a while and then we went down for a meal and some free time before we were locked up for the night. Even though I'm a big man myself, everyone else seemed bigger, and covered with threatening-looking tattoos. I wandered about feeling completely lost and alone in an aggressive, alien world. I still thought that after a couple of days they would realize it hadn't been my fault, that it had been Dad's, and then they would let me out. I just had to hold on till then. That night I felt I was back in the cellar under Cranbrook Street, trapped in an uncertain world, cuddling up to a cold brick wall, listening to the clunking of doors and the jangling of keys, having no idea if they would be coming in through the door at any moment.

The bed above my head began to shake and I wondered what my cellmate was up to. Was he masturbating? Did he have any tendencies? Had he ever hurt kids? He'd told me he was in for thumping his girlfriend, but what was he really in for?

I drifted off and was woken a bit later by a loud clunk and a shake of the bunk as my neighbour got down.

I lay listening as he relieved himself and broke wind
noisily.

After breakfast the next morning I went back to my cell
and found a prison guard waiting for me. When he turned
round I was shocked to see it was Angela's brother,
Adrian. He'd been working there for a couple of years but
I had no idea. He was the same age as me and we'd been
good friends at one time. The sight of a familiar face
cracked open the façade I'd been holding up since arriving and I started to cry, which set him off. It felt like he'd
come to save me.

'Matthew loves you, you know,' he said. 'He's always
wanted to see you. No one blames you for this, Stuart.
I know you've had a lot of problems but you're a good
lad. I'll always think of you as my brother-in-law,
despite what happened with Angela. You hurt her and
she wants to punish you by keeping the children from
you. I don't agree with a lot of things, but I keep them
to myself. Just try to hang in there, don't get any crazy
ideas. The truth will come out; everything will be OK.
I've had to tell them here that I know you, so there's a
very good chance they'll have to move you. But I'm
going to try and pull a couple of strings – not that
I've got many. The closest for your family would be
Forest Bank in Manchester. It's not a bad prison; it's
not a Strangeways. I'll try to get you sent there if you
have to move.'

He spent about twenty minutes with me, just talking, and I felt so much better at the end of it. I told him I wasn't too keen on my cellmate.

'There's a good lad downstairs called John,' he said. 'I'll get you moved down there.'

Everyone knew what I was in for, even before I got there, because it had been all over the TV and papers. I was surprised how many people came up and shook my hand, telling me I did the right thing, that they had suffered abuse when they were kids and they could understand why I'd flipped. It can't be any coincidence that so many people who are abused during childhood end up in prison.

The next night I was still in the same cell and I heard the movements start above me again. I was afraid to speak up, but I was more afraid of sexual activity going on near me. I felt I was being terrorized.

'I don't know what you're doing up there, pal,' I blurted out, 'but my head's fucked here and I can't handle stuff. If you start fucking masturbating I'll stab your fucking arms.'

'What you on about? I'm doing nothing.'

I felt it was important to get the upper hand quickly in prison. I wanted to be in control of what went on around me; I couldn't handle the feeling of being out of control.

Even though the food was foul, I was still getting hungry and I worked out that you couldn't be too late in the queue or you ran the risk of them running out of everything. When my cellmate and I went down for our tea on the second afternoon, the guy behind the serving hatch gave me a load of fish and some beans. I wanted some bread but they were down to the last loaf, the surface already littered with empty plastic wrappers. The guy in front of me picked up all that was left, a great fistful.

'Here, pal,' I said, 'can I have some of that bread there?'

'No, that's my bread.'

'What do you mean, that's your bread?'

'It's my bread.'

'I want a fucking slice of bread. Give me one. You've got about eight slices there.'

'No, it's my bread.'

The thread of self-control I'd been hanging on to snapped. I hurled my plate of food at the wall and booted the guy, screaming and shouting like a madman. Everyone else averted their eyes and moved away. Eventually I turned and walked away, shouting, 'Fucking wankers! I hate this fucking place!'

I sat down at one of the far tables, put my head in my hands and wept. It all seemed so unfair. I didn't think I'd done anything wrong and I had been thrown into this system without having anything explained to me. I was entitled to a life and they were trying to take mine away from me. I was a man now; I didn't have to take it like I did when I was a kid.

I sensed someone was approaching and looked up. It

was one of the screws. 'Here, lad,' he said, giving me some tobacco, 'get yourself a smoke.'

I was puzzled as to why I was being rewarded for bad behaviour. Another guy appeared behind him and I recognized him as being from the servery. He was carrying a plate loaded with the biggest pile of food I'd ever seen, far more than they had had in their serving dishes a few minutes before.

'Here, pal, get that down yer neck.'

I guess word about my past had started to spread around the wing and people were beginning to feel sympathy for me. From then on I was constantly being told by other prisoners that they didn't think I should be in there. The funny thing about prison is that although everyone is always claiming they're innocent of whatever they've been convicted of, other prisoners and screws always assume everyone is guilty. So it was a great boost to me that so many of them didn't think I deserved to be inside.

That night I was swapped around to be with John, who turned out to be a good guy. We had two separate beds instead of bunk beds and a much bigger cell. There was a proper private area for the toilet and everything was much cleaner. I felt far more relaxed. John was very open and seemed happy to talk about virtually anything.

On the third afternoon I was there Tracey managed to get in to see me. I'd been missing her so much it was like a physical pain. Seeing her lifted all the worries off my heart and I just stood there, hugging her, crying and telling her how sorry I was about the way things had turned out. The fresh start we'd been planning in Wales now seemed a distant memory. I was also beginning to worry about how young and inexperienced Ash Halam was. After all, he was just a duty solicitor, and I was beginning to grasp that this was going to be a murder trial. I felt I wanted to have someone who'd handled cases like mine before. I asked Tracey to ask around and she came back with a man called Padhee Singh, who was with the biggest firm of solicitors in Manchester.

She told me about the press coverage, which had been just as sensational as you would expect – the journalists describing the respectable old council worker in Wales whose stepson had driven over from Manchester and battered him to death. Even the local Mayor and Mayoress had come forward to have their pictures taken and to vouch for what a respectable member of the community Dad was. The fact that he'd been to prison for abusing Christina and Shirley seemed to have been forgotten. They wanted him to be the innocent victim in the story, and me the brutal young murderer in the black BMW.

My new cellmate John suggested I get a job, so I wouldn't have to spend so much time banged up in the cell. There was a lady officer on and I asked her if she had any jobs going.

'Yeah,' she said, 'you can get all these behind their doors now, it's bang-up.'

'Is that a job, yeah?'

'Yeah.'

I started walking round like a kid asking people to get behind their doors, not having a clue that she had just made it up on the spot: because I was a big guy she was using me to do her job for her. People were sticking their heads out. 'Get your heads behind the doors,' I told them, in all innocence, having no idea just how danger-ous it was. The funny thing was, they did do what I said. I guess my size, coupled with the fact that they knew I'd hammered a man to death, was giving me the upper hand I'd already realized I needed.

John gave me some good bits of advice. 'You need to stop calling the screws "sir" all the time, pal,' he said. 'You're sticking out a bit.'

'What do you mean?'

'Well, nobody's going to have a go at you because look at the size of you, but it would be better to call them "boss".'

'Why?'

'You just don't call them "sir". They're no better than you. They call you by your second name, don't they?'

He also told me there was a gym where we could go for an hour every so often and I signed up. As soon as I got there I could see there wasn't enough equipment to go round and I ran over to a bench. Another guy put his hand on it at the same time.

'What are you doing?' I asked.

'I'm here,' he said.

'I just got here.'

'No you didn't.'

I shoved him. 'Look, pal, you want to start something here you're gonna come off second best, but if you want to work with me we'll train together.'

For a second it looked like it was going to develop into a fight, but then he moved away and did something else. All the time there was this volatile feeling in the air, like things could explode at any moment.

The lack of privacy was hard. Even though I was comfortable with John, it would alarm me when he would just drop his trousers in front of me without any self-consciousness; it brought back bad memories – just like the way the sound of a man clearing his throat of phlegm, preparing to spit, reminded me of Dad spitting into his hand to lubricate himself when he masturbated or penetrated me. When I had gone to the gym on the outside I had always made sure I changed before I went and came home to shower. It had always been a problem, even at school. I never wanted to shower with the other guys. Nakedness frightened me and I didn't take a shower all the time I was in Altcourse because there was no privacy. People used to shit in the showers too, because some of the heroin addicts weren't able to control their bowels.

Tracey was coming to see me every day, and Mum came, and Christina, although she was so upset she just kept crying all the time. On one occasion when Tracey got there to sign in the guard said, 'Haven't they told you, love? He's been shipped up to Broadmoor.' Tracey immediately burst into tears. 'It's all right, love,' he said. 'I was only joking.' Dad would have appreciated that sort of humour. Another time they came to tell me that my dad was there to see me. I felt the blood draining from me. Was I going insane? Was he not dead? Was he coming after me? It turned out it was Trevor, who must have told them he was my stepdad.

The whole family had had to give long statements to the police and to the child protection team as everyone tried to piece together the extent that we had all been abused. They were obviously shocked to discover that I'd been keeping so much to myself over the years. They all knew that I'd had a lot of batterings because they'd seen them happen, and there had been all the abuses he'd done to us together, like watching the movies and reading the magazines, but they had never realized the extent of what he'd been doing to me whenever he got me on my own. I was equally horrified as I started to learn more details of some of the things he'd done to Shirley and Christina, which they'd never mentioned to me.

Mum also talked about things she had seen or he had made her do, which showed that she had been as much a victim of his cruelty and perverted appetites as the rest of us. Every day seemed to bring more and more revelations as the police and my new solicitors struggled to find out everything that had gone on in the past which might have led up to the terrible moment when I grabbed the hammer and fought back. At the same time the police were uncovering all about my life around the clubs, associating with known gangsters and drug dealers, being part of the world of the doormen. They were trying to prove that I had taken the hammer with me, because Trevor had lost one just like it, which would have shown that the killing was premeditated and not self-defence at all.

It was hard for my family and friends to get to Liverpool, so I was relieved when my transfer to Forest Bank in Salford came through. Despite being really pleased, I was also worried about having to travel all the way there in the sweatbox, frightened at the thought of being in such a confined space for so long. At first I refused to get into it, worried that if I had a panic attack in there and kicked off it would go on my report and I would begin to look like a madman, someone who was capable of killing a man with a hammer in cold blood. I could then end up in a psychiatric prison like Ashworth or Broadmoor and I knew that once you were in a place like that you were likely never to get out. No psychiatrist wants to take the risk of signing you off as safe and letting you back out into the world.

'I'm not getting on,' I said to the half-dozen prison officers encircling me.

'You're gonna have to get on the van,' the one in charge said.

'Well, you can try getting me on the van,' I said, 'but I'll kick off and I can't be responsible for what will happen. I don't want to hurt anybody but I feel panicky today and I can't cope with a confined space. So please don't make me.'

I heard the crackle of a radio. 'Can you send Big Gareth down to the reception area.'

I knew Big Gareth because he used to work on the doors in Chester and knew some of the lads I knew. As his name suggested, he was a big guy, the same size as me.

'You all right, mate?' he asked when he arrived.

'Yeah,' I said.

'What's up?'

'They want to give me a lift on the bus, but I ain't going on no fucking bus.'

'If you don't want to go on the bus that'll do for me, that's fine.'

'What are we going to do then?' one of the other screws asked.

'Well, what can you do? What's up with him?'

'He says he's claustrophobic and he might kick off.'

'I'm not trying to be funny,' I said, 'but I'm feeling volatile today.'

'We'll have to leave you here then,' Gareth said, taking a packet of fags out of his pocket and passing me one. 'But it means you won't get to Forest Bank. Isn't there any way you can do this? You'll be better off over there than here. If you stay here I might be able to get the psychiatrist to write you a letter and they'll have to take you up in a car with a couple of screws, but I don't know how long that will take.' He passed me the remains of his packet of cigarettes. 'There's some fags there, give it a few minutes and have a think. There's no way I'm going to be trying to manhandle you on here, and I don't think this lot intend to or they wouldn't have radioed through for me.'

The nice thing about Altcourse was that it was privately run by Group 4 Security, and the screws didn't have the same attitude problems that I knew existed in some of the old state-run prisons. By the time Gareth came back the nicotine had calmed me down a bit.

'I'm going to try to go on,' I said.

They didn't cuff me as they usually did, just let me walk on, sit down and breathe deeply.

'Yeah,' I said after a few minutes, 'all right.'

'All right, kid,' Gareth said. 'You've got fags, haven't you?'

'Yeah.'

'No problem. You take care of yourself. Everything is going to be all right.'

Nice bloke, Gareth. On the radio Sonique was singing 'I am free', and for a moment I felt that whatever they did to me, there was still a little part of me that was free; I was free of Dad because he had finally gone, taking so much of the fear I'd been living under with him. Through the small window I caught familiar glimpses of Manchester and Salford and I felt like I was going home. I'd only been at Altcourse a week and already it was beginning to feel like it had been another dream.

Chapter Fifteen

KICKING OFF

*F*orest Bank was another private nick, very clean, very tidy, floors polished until they shone. It looked a lot better than Altcourse.

I had to go through all the usual formalities and then I heard the words, 'Through here, Howarth. You're going to be strip-searched.'

'What do you mean, strip-searched?' I felt the familiar sense of panic rising, memories flashing back. I was going to have to strip in front of strange men? Have them examine me? The terror I had thought I was now free of returned like a juggernaut in the stomach.

'I'm frightened,' I admitted. 'I was abused as a kid.'

'We'll be as quick as possible.'

There was no way they were going to let me off. It was procedure. I was going to have to do exactly as they told me, just like I always had to do for Dad. There was a correct procedure to be followed: top off, top back on. Shoes and socks off, trousers off, boxers off, everything turned inside out and searched. Then I had to squat down so that anything I might have been trying to hide in my rectum would fall out. The two screws were professional and detached; they'd probably done it a thousand times. But I still felt humiliated and abused.

A lot of the inmates came up to say hello once I was in my cell and to ask if I had drugs. It seemed a pretty friendly place. Although there were bunks in the cell I was on my own, and the place was spotless, with a television and everything. They would play DVDs for us at weekends. The first I saw was *The Green Mile*, about a guy in prison.

'There's been a bit of bullying going on here,' one of the lads told me. 'Might be all right now you're here.'

'Why?'

'Bullies don't tend to bully when there's a big guy on the wing.'

There was a big black guy called Junior wandering around the wing, nearly seven feet tall with hands like shovels, shouting and having a go at people. The gossip was that he was knocking off one of the women screws, a blonde. He'd been a major crack dealer in Birmingham and some competitors had set on him and ripped off his dreadlocks, leaving him bald and patchy. I thought that if I was going to have any trouble that would be where it would come from. Altcourse had taught me that if I wanted to get on inside, I had to be prepared to fight, which I was.

The wing manager came to see me the next day and I discovered we had a lot of mutual friends in the body-building world. I felt comfortable talking to him, like I'd found a father figure.

'Do you want to work while you're here?' he asked.

'Yeah, I've never not worked in my life.'

'Do you want a job as a cleaner?'

'I'd love a job as a cleaner.'

'OK, then maybe we'll see if we can get you a job on the servery.'

I wondered if Adrian had already put in a word for me. I was given the ground floor to clean, mopping it and going over it with a buffer each day. I had to strip the polish off twice a week and reapply it. No wonder the place was so gleaming clean.

I had no trouble making friends, and I kept my eye on Junior. On my second day there I was mopping and I heard him having a falling out with another lad. He was wearing shorts, which I knew wasn't allowed on that floor. The screws were in their office and obviously didn't want to be involved. I kept on mopping with my head down, putting my mop in the bucket to pull it towards me each time I moved on. One time I misjudged it and tipped the bucket over, sending the dirty water across the floor. Junior started laughing and I've always had trouble with people mocking me, ever since Dad used to take the mickey about me being ugly, having 'Spock ears' and all the rest. I looked up.

'What are you fucking laughing at?'

'Fucking thick you are, mate,' he sneered.

'What do you mean, I'm thick?'

'You're a thick Manc. Look at you.'

'If I'm a thick Manc,' I said, 'you must be one thick Brummie. Have you seen the state of your head? You're like a fucking patchwork quilt. Is it like that on the rest of your body?'

'I've got hair, I've got hair!'

'You fucking prick,' I said, and at that he dropped his shorts and flashed everything at me, shaking his old man.

I threw the mop down with a crash and ran at him at full tilt, surprised to see he was already backing off. 'Come on, you fucking big black cunt!'

He dived into his cell and I followed him, grabbing hold of him. He immediately squatted down on the floor to protect himself.

'Fucking fight me, you bastard.'

But he wouldn't retaliate. I couldn't let it go because I knew he would have known I'd been abused and by doing that he was taking the piss, but I couldn't hit him if he wasn't going to defend himself, so I just gave him a load of verbal and pushed him away.

'Is it over now then, mate?' he asked. 'Is it forgot about?'

As I walked out of the cell I could hear the sound of jangling keys as the screws finally decided to come and see what was going on.

'Howarth, what are you doing in that cell?'

'Nothing, just having a laugh and joke.'

'Right, get on with your job.'

Word spread quickly. Junior was supposed to be the big man, running the wing, but everything had changed in a few seconds. People started coming up to me: 'Fucking nice one, mate. He's been shoving everyone about, the big soft twat. You stand up to him and he's shitting himself.'

The next day Junior was shipped out. I suppose in a way I became the main man on the wing at that moment. I wouldn't allow any bullying and I was promoted to the servery, which meant I got first crack at the food, which was far better than at Altcourse. They even gave us cakes and choc-ices and biscuits.

Tracey would come to see me and would write me a letter each day; she gave me a real feeling of hope, faith that things were going to be all right. I was taking my anti-depressants every morning and life was ticking along OK. My solicitors were also coming in most days. The only problem with visits was that they were supposed to strip-search me every time afterwards, although most of the screws realized how much it upset me and didn't bother. I was getting on with everyone and going to the gym regularly, writing letters to Tracey, Mum and Christina all the time, improving my health by being off the drugs.

One young lad tried to give me a hard time when he came in. It started with him shouting at a small lad who was the laundry orderly; then he started staring me in the face, demanding a cigarette. I knew I had to nip it in the bud, so I followed him into his cell after he'd picked up his dinner and faced him down. He hurled his plate of food at me, sending it everywhere. I grabbed him and felt a pain in my arse, like I'd banged into the door. I got him in a grip and let him know that I could have hurt him a lot more if I'd chosen to, and left the cell as I heard the jangle of approaching keys. Only when I got back to my cell did I discover that he'd stabbed me in the backside with his plastic fork, snapping the prongs off.

I obviously hadn't warned him hard enough because other people told me he was going round saying he was going to slash me up. We weren't allowed razor blades, but I'd managed to get some out of the safety razors they gave me. I went back to his cell and threw one down in front of him.

'What's that for?' he wanted to know.

'You're saying you want to slash me up. Go ahead, be my guest.'

'I've not said nothing.'

'Yeah you have.' I rolled up my sleeves and showed him the scars on both my arms. 'But you need to know that I did these to myself. If I can do that to myself, imagine what I could do to you.'

'All right, all right, leave it.'

A few hours later he was moved off the wing.

Christina had been to the police and told them about the paedophile friend of Dad's from the rough family in Smallshaw Lane who used to babysit us when we moved to Cranbrook Street, and how he used to abuse her. All the old skeletons that I had buried deep in my memory in order to be able to keep going seemed to be coming to the surface at once. At the time I'd thought it was just me he was doing it to and I was amazed to find out she'd been suffering exactly the same treatment. The police came in to get a statement off me, to see if they could put together a prosecution. It brought back some bad memories, but I liked the idea that he was going to be called to account for what he'd done.

Other police came in to tell me that they'd searched Dad's house and found all sorts of sex aids and blow-up dolls and pornographic videos. They found that he'd been making secret films through a hole in the wall of family members he had invited to use the shower in his house.

Trevor had found his lump hammer by then, which helped my argument that I had never taken it with me, that it had been Dad's hammer I had just grabbed in self-defence. Everyone kept showing me files of information and I started to read even more about how my sisters had been abused. Although I had always had a good idea what had happened, it was still hard to actually see it in black and white and to be faced with the true ferocity of the attacks they suffered.

There was no separate wing for sex offenders at Forest Bank, so I was constantly aware that I might be mixing with paedophiles and rapists without knowing it. 'Most of the nonces are in the block,' other inmates reassured me when I voiced my worries, referring to the segregation area. All the lads on the wing were very respectful. I would tell them when I was having a shower and ask them to respect my privacy because I was a bit touchy about it, and they always did that.

There was a big fat lad on the wing from Wigan who used to make me laugh. He was about twenty-three stone and I used to bench-press him to entertain the other guys. He was called Mellon, and he used to come into the cell to talk to me. He knew a bit about my past and used to ask me a lot of questions.

'Not surprised you killed him,' he said. 'Sounds like a right twat. You shouldn't be in here.'

One day he wasn't on the wing and I was told he'd gone to court. It was only then that some of the other lads from Wigan told me he was inside for battering a little girl, pissing on her and abusing her. I was furious that they'd let me have a laugh and joke with a man who did things like that. I felt like Mellon had been mocking me all the time I'd been talking about my past, that he'd had me over royal. I guess one of the reasons he'd become friendly with me was because he was frightened of what I would do if I ever found out.

He didn't come back on to our wing that night, but I knew he would be in the medical section the next morning when I went for my tablets. I had a Scouse friend who was going to help me and I would get him to go outside and get a light off the screw and block his view. I was pretty sure I could have a word with Mellon underneath the camera, so the other screws wouldn't know what was going on either.

As I walked into the room he was there. There were

screws everywhere and I knew I shouldn't do anything, but I couldn't control myself.

'You took the piss out of me,' I said and hit him, sending him flopping to the ground. The screws whisked me back to my wing.

'What's going on?' they wanted to know.

'He hit me.'

'We were there, Stuart. He didn't hit you.'

They sent me back up to get my medication and when I came out about twenty minutes later I saw Mellon, surrounded by four or five screws and wearing a neck brace. They pulled him to one side to let me by with the two screws escorting me.

Later that morning the wing manager came to see me and I knew I'd disappointed him. 'How could you do that in front of the security manager?' he wanted to know.

'Who's the security manager?'

'He was stood right there, watching you.'

I tried to explain how it felt to come up against people like Mellon. 'He was in this cell, sharing coffee and tea and fags with me. You knew what he'd done and you put him into my environment. How does that make me feel? I hate him because he took the piss out of me, because he hurt a little girl and because I've shared personal information with him.'

'OK,' he said eventually. 'Well, unless he says anything, this won't go any further. But don't do anything like that again, OK?'

Obviously Mellon didn't say anything.

I was beginning to know who my real friends were, because they were the ones who came in to see me at visiting times. There was a couple I'd met through my work at the electricity board. Their names were Sue and Geoff Hadfield. Geoff was a farmer who ran a successful wood recycling business on his land. I'd been sent to help them develop the electrical side of the site and we'd got on well. Geoff was a lovely man, the sort of bloke I would have loved to have had as a father. I wrote to them to apologize for not finishing their development work and explained what had happened. Sue wrote back, shocked and mortified, and told me what a fantastic guy I was, always coming in to work with a smile on my face. 'We always thought you were so happy-go-lucky and we're devastated to hear the truth of your story. If there is anything we can do to help just ask.'

It made me cry when I read it. For the first time in my life all sorts of people were starting to show me that they really cared.

The big problem in prison is always money. I was still being paid my salary since I was only on remand, and I was allowed to transfer thirty pounds a week into my prison account. It's surprising how quickly you can spend thirty pounds when you're paying inflated prison prices for toiletries and tobacco, so I needed to have other income. Prisoners who had already been convicted were only allowed fifteen pounds a week, so they always wanted to get their hands on the canteen stuff that remand prisoners could afford more of. But convicted prisoners were given more phone credits, so they would trade them, and it was the phone credits that I wanted.

Drugs are a huge business in prisons. Ninety per cent of that drug use is heroin. Because it's opium based it's out of your system within twenty-four hours, whereas cannabis can take up to thirty days. So everyone ended up chasing the dragon, sucking up the smoke to escape from the reality of their lives inside. In a half-hearted attempt to keep the drug-taking in the prison under control, the authorities would occasionally get prisoners' piss tested. If they were caught they could get an extra thirty days on their sentence. Because I was taking no drugs, my piss was clean, making it a valuable commodity to sell or barter. I would piss into the plastic snappy bags that had held our teabags and keep it warm on the hot pipe in the room. When the screws came round to do tests other inmates would give me half an ounce of tobacco in exchange for a bag. They'd take it into the test room with them and put it into the bottle.

I had no problems at Forest Bank until Tracey's brother, Paul, bumped into an officer from the prison called Frank. They used to go to school together.

'Do you know Stuart Howarth?' Paul asked.

'Stuart's on my wing,' Frank said. 'He's all right he is. I look after him. Whatever Stuart wants, Stuart gets.'

This was news to me. I used to say hello to him because he'd told me he knew Paul, but he never looked after me in any way. Paul, however, believed him and went and bought 200 fags for Frank to take in to me. A couple of days later Tracey told me about the fags.

'I don't need anything, Tracey,' I said. 'I've got enough money. Tell Paul not to go messing things up for me here. I'm OK.'

The next day Frank came up to me. 'What fags do you smoke?' he asked.

'I'll smoke anything.'

Paul kept getting Tracey to ask if I'd got the fags yet. He even asked me himself once on the phone when I was talking to Tracey at work. I didn't want to talk to him about it; I knew my calls were being recorded.

A few days later I was on my way to the visiting area to see Tracey, making my way down the long corridor, going through all the gates as usual. When I got to one of them Frank was there. He had bruising all over his face and big swollen eyes, and I got a feeling everyone was acting funny around me.

'You all right, Mr Thompson?' I asked, but he didn't reply.

When I got to Tracey I discovered that Paul had bumped into Frank in a club and asked what had happened to the fags.

'I've given them to him.'

Knowing he was lying, Paul had battered him there and then in the club. Frank had since gone to the authorities and told them that I was trying to get him to take fags in, threatening to have him beaten up if he refused. This was another complete lie.

Wanting to defuse the situation as quickly as possible I went to the wing manager and told him that whatever was going on with Frank was nothing to do with me. He told me to write down everything I knew about the situation. I said OK, but on my way back to the cell I thought I shouldn't do anything without talking to my solicitors. The problem was it was Sunday and I knew I wouldn't be able to get hold of them.

Later that day a screw came to my cell. 'Howarth, have you got that statement written?'

'No,' I admitted. 'I just need to speak to my solicitors in case I incriminate myself.'

'He wants it written today.'

'I'm not writing it today.'

He went off to report back and I felt a familiar wave of panic gripping me. A while later two screws came back.

'Right, Howarth, you're either going to get this thing written or you're going to the segregation unit.'

'You can put me in the hospital if you want,' I said, 'but I'm not going in that segregation unit because it's full of paedophiles and sex offenders. I refuse to go down that area.'

'Unless he gets that statement that's where we're taking you.'

'Please, what's the rush? Tell him he can have it tomorrow. Please don't take me down there.'

'Hang on a minute.'

They plodded off again and returned a few minutes later. 'No, he says he wants it in the next twenty minutes.'

I'd been having some counselling with a woman called Ruth, who had been really helping me. 'Go and talk to Ruth,' I said. 'I've had a lot of conversations with her and she'll explain the situation to you about why I don't want to go down there, and what it might do to me. It terrifies me to think what those guys have done before they came in here.'

I would never have been able to stay sane if I'd been in a cell next to someone masturbating, imagining in my head what might be going on in theirs.

The screws left again, locking my cell door behind them. I paced up and down, trying to keep calm. A few minutes later I heard a lot of activity outside and I peered out through the window. Everyone else was being locked up in their cells and I knew what that meant: they were coming to get me.

'Stuart,' a friend shouted, 'what's going on?'

'They want to put me in the fucking seg, with all the dirty fucking beasts. There's no way I'm going in there.'

'Calm down, Stuart,' someone shouted.

'Take it easy, Stuart!' came from someone else.

'Go wherever they say.'

The frustration was knotting me up inside. I couldn't calm down; I could only explode. I knew I would rather kill myself than go into that place. I had two safety razors hidden away and I pulled them from their hiding place, fumbling to get the blades out. The noise was getting closer outside. The shouting died away and it all went quiet. I could hear them talking downstairs. I looked out the window and saw they were all in their riot gear: boots, shin pads, shields, helmets, and a camera.

The flap on the outside of the door snapped shut and I couldn't see any more. More voices and then the flap opened again and the camera was there.

'Right, Howarth,' a voice announced. 'We are now going to be escorting you to the segregation unit. We'll be coming in that cell shortly and we want you to come quietly.' The camera moved away and a big fat screw, whom I'd never liked, looked in.

'You're not fucking coming in here!' I screamed, brandishing the blades. 'See these? I'll fucking slash you. I'll stab you. I don't care. There's no way I'm going in there.'

He laughed at me. 'Do you think that's going to stop us?'

'Well, come in then,' I challenged him.

'We can wait all night,' he laughed. 'We aren't going anywhere.'

'Please.' I tried one last time. 'Lock me in one of the cells in medical.'

He seemed to be deliberately winding me up, as if he wanted to see what would happen.

'I'm not going fucking nowhere,' I yelled and started slashing at my arms, crying all the time. 'You bastards, look what you've made me do now.'

The blades cut in deep and wide, much worse than I'd ever done before. Blood sprayed across the room. I sank down on to the bed. I was wearing shorts and there was blood all over my legs, running down and puddling on the floor.

I could hear the stirrings of panic outside the door now.

'Put the blades down, Howarth!'

'Stuart!' I heard a woman's voice and recognized it as belonging to one of the women in the medical centre. She was an older woman who had always been nice to me. 'Look at the state of you. Please put the blades down. Let us come in. We can't come in while you're still holding the blades.'

'Look what they've done,' I cried. 'Why did they have to do this? They all know what I've been through. Please don't take me to seg. Please take me to medical.'

'All right, sweetheart,' she said, 'but please let me have those blades. Please push them under the door. You're going to bleed to death.'

She shouted at the men around her, demanding to know why they hadn't come to get her earlier. The room was swimming and their voices were becoming distant.

'All right,' I said, my strength beginning to slide away, 'as long as you look after me.'

I managed to get to the door and slid the blades out. The door opened and she came in, wrapping towels around my wounds to try to stem the bleeding. Behind her I could see the faces of the screws, looking shocked

and bewildered. I suppose they'd thought they were dealing with a hard man, the main man on the wing, and
instead they found themselves dealing with a frightened
little boy in a grown-up's body.

She got me on to my feet and walked with me to
the medical wing, with them all around, their camera
still filming.

'This is Frank Thompson's fault,' I said. 'I hope you
get this on the tape. This is nothing to do with me. I didn't
ask for any cigarettes. I didn't ask my brother-in-law to
do anything. I was doing my best to get on here.'

A guy who had never stitched anyone before did my
stitches, but the thread kept pulling through the skin.
The woman who had rescued me seemed so sad as
she watched.

'I'm so sorry. I wish I could take you home with me, love.
I've known you, Stuart. You've never been an ounce of
trouble. If anything the place has gone quiet since you've
been here. There's a lot less bullying going on. Why did
it come to this? Why didn't they come and get me first?'

When the wing manager came to see me I was still
caked in my own blood. He looked at me and sighed.

'I don't know, Stuart,' he said. 'You're a silly lad, aren't
you?'

'I might be a silly lad, boss, but I told you. I begged
you not to put me in there. You've done this to me
because you wanted that statement. I've done nothing
wrong. It's all because you've got an officer who isn't
working by the book.'

'I've done the best I can for you, Stuart.'

'You've done very well by me up till now,' I admitted, 'but you've mishandled this.'

'Well, what I've come to tell you is that you're being shipped out and you're going to Strangeways. I'm telling you now, Strangeways is the worst jail you could ever hope to go to.'

He didn't have to tell me that. Everyone in the Manchester area had heard about Strangeways – a traditional prison run on traditional rules. I knew that many of the officers in there were staunch supporters of the National Front. I'd heard about the racism that went on, the squalor and dirt. I didn't want to go there but he had decided I was trouble and I had to be shipped out.

Chapter Sixteen

STRANGEWAYS

racey cried when I saw her the next day in the hospital block. 'Please promise me you will never do anything like that again,' she begged.

'Tracey, I would rather have died than gone in there.'

'But things were going so well, you were looking better than I've ever seen you, and you go and do something like this. I don't understand why.'

The hospital section was also the young offenders' section and the kids used to play football outside. Some of the younger ones were smashing up everything and kicking off against one another. They would jeer at me through the window of my cell. There were no curtains so I couldn't get away from them: 'Look at yer, yer fucking self-harmer! What's up with yer?'

When the time came to move me I was double cuffed to a screw, and chained to him as well. By the time we got to the transport I had an escort of eight screws. All of them travelled with me to Strangeways, a towering, red brick monster of a jail squatting in a run-down area close to the centre of Manchester, its watchtower visible for miles around.

The moment I walked in, the contrast to Forest Bank was terrible. Instead of shining, polished floors there was rubbish and pigeon shit everywhere. Everything was ugly and run down, scruffy and dirty. All the screws looked older and their uniforms were more formal and official looking. Two of them took me off the bus and marched me in.

'Right, Howarth, you're at fucking Strangeways now. You're no longer at Forest Gump. This is a proper jail. If you fuck about with us you'll get in trouble. Do you hear me? We run this jail, not you, and this is how we start. Go and sit in that room there.'

'Look, boss, I'm trying ...'

'I didn't ask you to fucking speak. Go and sit in that room there.'

Some of my scars were still bleeding and my stitches were rough and frayed. I must have looked like a complete psychopath. They left me for a while and then I heard the keys outside.

'Right, Howarth,' the guard barked, throwing open the door. 'You're going to the block.'

'I'm not going to the block. Please, I've done nothing wrong. If you tell me I'm going to the block I'm going to kick off.'

'Oh, you're going to kick off, are you?'

'I'm begging you, please don't send me to the block.' I wasn't sure what the block was, but I did know it wasn't good and I'd heard that they stripped you naked and left you on a mat.

He slammed the door and disappeared for a while. When he came back he told me I wasn't going to the block, I was going to K Wing.

'So, you're a lucky lad, aren't you?'

I was taken in front of the doctor who ordered me to be put under suicide watch, and then I was escorted to a windowless cell, hot as a sauna, where I was left with about forty other dangerous-looking guys with no food or water. The toilet in the corner stank and there was no toilet paper.

There were a few attempts at conversation, but no one really felt much like talking.

'How'd you get them scars?'

'Razor blades.'

'What you in for?'

'Murder.'

'Fucking hell.'

Five hours later they threw open the door. It seemed that the screws did things when they felt like it; there was none of the efficiency of Forest Bank here.

'Right, K Wing lads.'

About thirty of us stood up and filed out. The place was enormous. We seemed to be walking forever down noisy, filthy corridors and climbing staircases, kicking our way through discarded plastic and scavenging pigeons, our footsteps echoing off the bare walls. There were strip-searches, with no attempt at modesty or dignity,

everything was taken off us, leaving us naked and vulnerable and humiliated. One of the rules of strip-searching
is that the prisoner should be able to keep his genitals
covered at all times, but they didn't bother with that.
I tried to tell them that I'd been abused, but I was just
met with deaf ears and disinterested stares. Maybe they
hear it all the time. One screw actually put his hand on
my abdomen and told me I was fat. The comment didn't
bother me, but the touch of his palm made me want to
scream with fear.

There were around two hundred men on the wing.
We were all put together into a room and told to wait.
As I sat there, listening to all the unfamiliar noises going
on around me, another prisoner walked past the open
door, stopped and walked back, peering in.

'Stu?'

It was a guy called Jimmy who used to live a few doors
away from us in Smallshaw Lane. He was a fair bit older
than me, but I remembered playing with him as a kid and
seeing him about from time to time after that. He had
actually been a friend of the guy I'd battered in the pub
the night of Shirley's funeral. The guy I hit had sent
Jimmy and a few lads down the next night to beat me
up, not realizing Jimmy knew me. 'Stuart, how are you
doing?' he'd asked when he saw it was me. He knew
Mum and he'd heard about our Shirley. There was no
way he was going to beat me up. We had a drink and a
chat instead. It was good to see his familiar face again
outside the cell. I poured out all my problems.

'I've seen you on TV and all,' he said, standing in the door of the cell. 'Leave it with me, I'll sort you out.'

I knew that if he was walking about he must have a job as an orderly of some sort, which meant he might be in a position to help me get settled in. In the meantime I was moved to the fourth floor. Netting had been strung between the floors so no one could throw themselves off the balconies. I was given a moth-eaten blanket, a sheet with shit stains on it and a set of plastics that had obviously been used to death already. The bowl looked like the ones Dad used to make us share with the dogs.

The cell looked like it hadn't been touched in twenty years, black with dirt, pigeons sitting on the windowsill. There was no tap or plug to the sink and the mattress was ripped and stained. I felt I had just plunged back into the very darkest years of my childhood. I was sharing the cell with another inmate, a scruffy-looking bloke, but by that stage I was just ready to sleep. I warned him not to move about too much in the night because it frightened me.

'I can't be responsible for how I react,' I explained.

Because I was on suicide watch the screws were meant to check on me every hour, although I think they only looked in about once a night. It was November by then and winter was getting a grip. The cell grew cold at night because the window wouldn't shut properly and there was only one hot pipe running through it. Sometimes the pigeons would barge their way in and shit on the beds.

As soon as everyone was locked up for the night and the screws had gone off the wing a riot of noise went up as people shouted to one another from cell to cell.

'What's going on?' I asked.

'Everyone's doing lines.'

He explained how inmates would pass things back and forth between the windows. They would unpick threads from the blankets, which was why they were so full of holes, tie them together with a weight on one end and the drugs they wanted to pass. They'd feed it out the window on the end of a broom handle or whatever they could get and it was passed down the line from one cell to the next. My cellmate was a heroin addict, so he would get heroin sent along to him from about ten cells away.

'Pass that line!' the shout would go.

'Pass the line!'

'Where's that fucking line?'

'What's going on?'

'If you're fucking about with my fucking gear I'm gonna fucking do yer as soon as this cell door opens.'

When his delivery finally made it he asked if I wanted some.

'No,' I said, 'I don't do it.'

He got some foil off a Kit-Kat and a pen top and lit the heroin, sucking up the smoke, dulling whatever pain he had in his head. I remembered that feeling so well from drinking and cocaine, but I didn't want to go back there, not when I needed to have all my wits about me. Eventually I made it into a shallow, dream-disturbed sleep.

'What time's breakfast?' I asked when we woke up, imagining the toast and cereal I'd got used to at Forest Bank.

'You have to get your breakfast the night before,' he told me, showing me the bowl of cereal and carton of milk he'd got.

It was impossible to work out what I was meant to be doing. The screws did nothing but shout and swear and I was dependent on other inmates to explain the system, but it was just a question of survival. By the time we got into the canteen for lunch the food had virtually gone. Jimmy was working behind the servery and slapped some carrots on my plate, then winked.

'Is that it?' I asked, looking at the screw.

'Yes, that is fucking it,' he snarled. 'Have you got a problem with that?'

'I'm fucking hungry. I've had no fucking breakfast.'

'Fucking move it, or I'll put you on report.'

By the time I got back to my cell I was in despair. The mixture of fear and hunger reminded me so much of my childhood. I didn't think I was going to be able to hold on to my sanity.

'Do you want something to eat?'

I looked up and Jimmy was standing in the door in his whites. He passed me a bowl with some chips and a sort of burger in it.

'You fucking gent, Jim.'

The next day I was moved down to the second floor to share with Jimmy and they gave me a job as a cleaner. I felt like I'd been saved by a guardian angel.

'Told you I'd fucking sort you out.' He grinned. 'You'll be all right with me. I've got a TV, a kettle. There's tea and coffee in that Tupperware box. I've done a lot of jail, I'll show you how it works. Uncle Jim's here now, he's going to look after you.'

The cell was still filthy with age, but Jimmy had done his best and at least it had a window that would shut. You were only allowed to have one pillow but Jimmy had got three on each bunk. The beds were made and the floor was polished. I immediately felt safer; I'd found myself a new father figure.

They kitted me out with a pair of overalls and some steel-capped boots. Cleaning at Strangeways was very different to Forest Bank, so much steelwork, brickwork and old floors where you had to get down on your knees and scrub. You had to climb on to the netting to polish in between the railings. In the servery I had to give out the bread and wash all the dirty pots up. The scars on my arms were still quite raw and sometimes bled, which worried me a bit when I was working in the filthy, slimy washing-up water, and when I saw the rats running around in the shadows carrying God knows what germs with them. But I didn't care how hard the work was, I just wanted to be busy and to keep my mind distracted from the thoughts and memories and fears that competed to overwhelm me.

There was no toast in Strangeways, and it's amazing how much you start missing little luxuries like that, especially when the normal food was so shit. Jimmy taught me how to make cheese on toast using an iron. He'd go to the office and tell them he needed to press his trousers for a visit the next day. He then secreted it in the cell, along with some greaseproof paper, and cooked us a little late-night snack – just the smell was enough to drive me wild.

He also sorted me out with a phone card so I could talk to Tracey. He phoned Mum himself to reassure her he was going to look after me. The attitude of the screws immediately seemed to change towards me, as if I'd proved myself to them simply by being a friend of Jimmy's. But they still needed to show that they were completely in control and had power over everybody. A couple of them let me know that they were regulars in Mum's pub and that they would look after me. One of them was a night watchman and every so often he would shove a newspaper underneath my door. Little gestures like that made a big difference. It made me think that perhaps I wasn't quite as naughty a boy as the system was trying to make me believe.

'You all right?' the night watchman would ask if we passed. 'I was in the pub last night. Your mum sends her regards.'

I felt a glimmer of hope returning; maybe everything would be all right in the end. I had all my case files with me in the cell and Jimmy and I would look through them together, trying to work out what was likely to happen once I got into court. When we got talking I told him about the babysitter who used to interfere with us. He knew him, because they'd been around the same age when we all lived in Smallshaw Lane.

'The dirty bastard,' he said. 'You know his son's in here, don't you?'

'Yeah?'

'You want to know something else that'll shock you?'

'What?'

'He's called Stuart.'

Had he chosen the name because of me? I didn't know what to make of it.

'Can you get to him?' I asked. 'He might know something about his dad. God, I hope he hasn't abused him too.' But the kid was released before Jimmy could get to him.

Tracey was able to get in to see me each day, and even though the screws tended to make nasty remarks to her, it was bearable as long as we got to see one another.

If inmates got to hear that anyone was in there for rape or child abuse, it was never long before they got beaten up, even if they hadn't been convicted; an accusation was enough. The place was so scary, so volatile with gangs and drugs, fights and beatings happening all the time, I could sense danger all around.

There was a young black lad who swore he was in for

assault, but whispers were beginning to go about that it was rape.

'You better get these rumours sorted out,' I told him when we were walking back from visiting time together one day, 'because if it comes out you are in here for rape you'll get done. You know that and I know that.'

I was working on the servery a few nights later, sweating in the heat. I saw the same black lad come through but thought nothing of it. A minute later the bells were ringing and the keys were jangling as the screws came running in shouting.

'Out the way! Out the way!'

I got a glimpse of the lad being taken out and there was blood everywhere. I thought no more about it, just kept serving up the dinners. Incidents like that were happening all the time.

A grey-haired security officer came in. 'Howarth! You! Out here!'

'Me, boss?'

'I'm not fucking speaking to anyone else. Out here now.'

There were two screws waiting and I was taken up to the office. 'What the fuck's going on with you and this black lad?'

'What black lad?'

'The rapist, you know the one. He's down in the hospital now. He's got a broken jaw. He's been slashed across the eye. Four lads have done him in the recess with their trays.'

'What's that got to do with me?'

'I'll tell you what that's got to do with you. He tells me the big lad on the servery with all the scars on his arms said something to him the other day about "You'd better sort it out in case you're a rapist". Whether he's a rapist or not, whether he's a nig-nog or not, we've got a job to do here. I looked at your file. I saw what you're in for. You've been abused and you've killed your stepfather. I might have bloody known you'd set this up.'

'I haven't set anything up. I was on the servery, working. How could it have been me?'

'There's more to this than meets the eye. I've done my damnedest to keep you on this wing. A lot of people are rooting for you. I do my best for you. You should be on E Wing; you're a potential lifer. You know you're getting life for what you've done, don't yer?'

'Boss, I've not done nothing. Why are you having a go at me?'

'Well, I'm telling yer. I've stuck my neck on the line for you, but you have to leave this wing. I know there's people here who know your mother, and Jimmy's a good lad. I've done my best to keep you on this wing but if you've gotta move you've gotta move.'

Yet again I was reminded how fragile my security was. At any moment I could be whisked away to another wing, full of unfamiliar and unpredictable new faces and away from the safety of Jimmy's influence.

Chapter Seventeen

DID YOU ENJOY IT?

*T*he chaplain started coming to see me, and it turned out she knew Seb. Seb had left Christina by then and had gone off and joined the God Squad after his accident. I didn't mind her coming to see me, and she blessed me in my cell. She gave me a Bible and said it would be nice to see me in church. I told her I was very frightened and still had a lot of issues I needed to talk about.

'I'll try to get you some counselling,' she promised.

A couple of days later I was introduced to a voluntary counsellor called Neil. I was escorted to his room and once we were alone he made me a cup of coffee in a real mug. Little gestures like that mean a lot when you're inside. I started to cry as I talked, and I noticed he wasn't writing anything down.

'I don't take notes,' he explained. 'That way no one else can ever get to use them against you. I will respect your privacy and whatever you tell me in this room will stay with me.'

I immediately felt comfortable with him and started seeing him once a week.

I came back to the cell one day to find Jimmy packing. 'Where are you going?'

'They're sending me on a course for alcoholics, to get me ready for going back outside.'

'Do you have to go? Can't you put it off?'

'No. Don't worry. I've been on them before. I'll be back in a couple of days.'

When a screw finally came to move me to E Wing with all the 'lifers' I was full of fear. I knew it would mean living among killers and violent people, and I never saw myself as being one of them, even if the authorities did. The wing was divided into two halves, and the only vacancy was on the maximum security side. I got a single cell, which I asked for, but I was in amongst the most hardcore prisoners now. It might have been a buzz to hang out with notorious gangsters in the clubs, but being trapped in prison with them was terrifying. Because many of them were preparing their cases in there they were allowed to have all the evidence they needed to go over for their defences, which meant there were some gruesome photographs and autopsy reports going about, which they would show off proudly, sometimes selling their trophies off to other ghouls.

'He's off 'is 'ead, isn't he?' one man chuckled to me over lunch one day, giving me a knowing nudge.

I looked down at the photo he was holding out for me and saw the head of his victim severed from its body. He told me he'd removed it with a hacksaw. Even though I averted my eyes, the image had already burned itself into my memory and would never leave.

There were only thirty or forty people on the wing and as soon as I arrived they asked me if I wanted a cleaning job. There were all sorts of rules left over from when the place was full of IRA men, like having to change cells every twenty-eight days in case you were trying to escape. I was excused that as I was a category B prisoner, despite being on that wing. Visitors also had to come right into the prison, which Tracey found very daunting, having to walk past men who would shout obscenities at her. My cell faced out over the street, so after she had been to visit I could run back up there and wave to her as she left, prolonging the visit a few moments longer, making it feel like we were still linked outside the confines of the visitors' room. She looked so tiny and far away in the bleak, empty streets that surround Strangeways.

There were far more screws everywhere on E Wing, many of them the hardest and meanest men in the service. The worst part for me was that they were constantly strip-searching us, before and after every visit. I'd noticed there was a sign on the wall instructing them on how to perform the searches, but they never bothered to follow the procedures or protect our privacy or dignity in any way. They were always particularly racist towards the black lads, making them squat and spread the cheeks of their arses while they just sat there eating their butties.

Sometimes they would make little comments. 'You're a big boy,' one would say to me. 'Been taking your steroids, have you?'

'Oh look,' another commented. 'Your balls are all shrivelled up.'

'Why do you have to say anything when I get undressed?' I asked. 'Why do you have to say anything at all?'

They just smirked.

No matter how often it happened I could never get used to it, never stop the feelings of being a small vulnerable boy again, trembling in expectation of a beating or a raping, remembering how Dad used to inspect me before he did things to me.

Padhee Singh and my barrister wanted me to have a psychiatric report because part of my defence was going to be manslaughter on the grounds of mental instability. I would come back from sessions with the psychiatrist, having been reliving the most terrifying and humiliating experiences of my childhood, talking about being raped and buggered, only to have to go through an invasive strip-search immediately afterwards as I was brought back on to the wing, having already been through one on my way out.

'Can I just have a moment, please, boss,' I would plead. 'Just to get my head together.'

'No. Get your fucking clothes off.'

I was starting to learn a lot about child abuse from the various counsellors and psychologists I was talking to, and the general consensus seemed to be that victims such as me came away from the experience suffering Post Traumatic Stress Disorder in much the same way as soldiers returning from active duty might. The fear and insecurity experienced on a battlefield in a war zone has a similar effect to being constantly brutalized and terrorized as a child. In a way it was comforting that the experts believed that all the things I saw as being my problems were in fact explainable and understandable, once it was known what I had been through. On the other hand it also made me very angry to think that all my unhappiness – and the unhappiness I caused in the lives of those I loved – had been brought about by the one man who was supposed to love and protect me, my dad.

The cell they gave me was a hole, with a window that wouldn't shut, no matter how hard I tried. The birds kept getting in, shitting over everything and stealing any food that I might manage to get.

I'd been receiving letters from Tracey every day, and suddenly they started to be delayed and I couldn't understand why.

'You all right, Cutie?' a screw asked one day, and the penny dropped. 'Cutie Face' was a pet name Tracey would use for me in my letters, and I would call her 'Tracey Doll'. Not only were they intercepting my mail, they didn't care if I knew it. The comments kept coming all the time, like playground taunts. I couldn't understand why they were treating me like that. Then my canteen supplies didn't turn up. I went down to the office to complain. I don't think I got aggressive, but I was definitely feeling frustrated. 'Fuck off back to your cell,' they told me.

The next thing I knew I'd been sacked from my cleaning job. They obviously wanted me to know that they were in charge and they could do whatever they liked to me. If I complained or tried to stand up for myself, things would just get worse. Yet again I felt like a helpless child, surrounded by unkind adults.

'Howarth!' a screw barked one evening. 'You've got a police visit tomorrow.'

I could sense dozens of pairs of ears pricking up around me. The last thing anyone in a maximum-security wing wants to hear is that one of their fellow inmates is going to be having a chat with the police. Who knows what subjects might come up in the course of the conversation? If the police were coming to see me, it meant there was a strong possibility I was a grass, the one thing that absolutely no one in a prison will tolerate. I had been warned not to discuss my case in the cells, for fear of being overheard; paranoia is everywhere in a prison. The police actually wanted to talk to me about the case they were building up against the abusive babysitter.

I was angry with the screw for putting me in such a dangerous situation, and I told him so. He couldn't have cared less. Sometimes they actually seemed to take pleasure in messing me about: turning up late when I had to be escorted to fetch my medication, or not turning up at all so I would miss one of my counselling sessions with Neil. They had complete power over my destiny, just like Dad had when I was a kid.

There was one screw in particular, I'll call him Smith, who seemed to have it in for me. He would do the strip-searching a different way each time, which was frightening and disorientating. If I had to take all my clothes off in front of another man I wanted it done impersonally, by the book.

'Don't you realize how threatening this is for me?' I asked, when I was being taken through for a visit with a friend.

'Just get your clothes off,' he snapped. 'We decide how things are done around here, not you.'

'But I was abused as a kid. Can't you imagine what it feels like to be abused by a fully grown man?'

'Why, did you enjoy it?'

'You what?' I couldn't believe I'd heard him right.

'You fucking heard. Did you like it?'

'Did I like it?' I couldn't stop the tears from coming. 'Did I fucking like it? Fuck off!'

'Come on,' he snapped, impatient with me now. 'Do you want your visit?'

'No, I don't want my fucking visit. Just get me out of here. Take me back on the wing.'

My overwhelming instinct was to attack him, to beat

him, to bite his smug face. I managed to hold it in, but I couldn't hold in the tears. I ran to the dividing gate and demanded that it be opened by the screw on the other side. I burst through it, screaming and shouting.

'I can't believe what he has just said to me!'

A senior officer appeared from nowhere with four screws, obviously nervous that I was about to kick off. The senior officer listened to my ranting for a moment and agreed that Smith was out of order. Another screw, who had witnessed the exchange, backed me up.

'He doesn't usually work on this wing,' the senior officer said, as if that excused him. 'But that was out of order. Do you want to make a complaint?'

'Yes, I want to make a complaint.'

'OK, come down to the office tomorrow and collect a form.'

This was my first experience of the endless business of trying to make complaints against prison officers: the forms that had to be filled in, the forms they would consequently lose, and the glowering hostility that I would be faced with. In the hope of channelling my fury, I decided to start keeping a diary from that date of all the things that happened to me inside Strangeways.

Someone must have believed I was in the right because I was given my job back the next day. But it didn't last long. Once you have made enemies in a place like Strangeways they can always find a way of getting to you. I was sweeping up on the wing when Smith came past.

'Howarth,' he said, 'you're nicked. Get behind doors.'

I threw my broom down in a fury. 'Why are you picking on me?'

They were putting me on 'basic' for some trumped-up charge of using foul language towards one of the female screws he was with as he walked past. Later we found out the two of them were having an affair.

'Basic' meant I would be locked behind my cell door all day, with no right to a TV and reduced visits. But the promised charge sheet never transpired, so I guess there were some officers there who knew that I hadn't done anything wrong and weren't going to allow my enemies a completely free rein to persecute me.

Neil gave me a lot of good advice, but the trouble with that was that a lot of the time that should have been spent talking about what had happened to me in my childhood was taken up with talking about the treatment I was now getting in jail.

Sometimes my mail would go missing. Or I would queue for an hour to get on the phone, and the moment I got through on my call they would cut the lines off.

'The phone's gone off, boss,' I'd complain.

'Nothing wrong with the phone, Howarth.'

I would then have to go to the back of the queue again and the phone times would be over by the time I got back to the front.

I was moved to a cell where the windows wouldn't shut at all and there was no mattress on the bed. The frequency of the strip-searches became ludicrous, sometimes as often as eight times in a day, sometimes four for just one visit. It seemed as if I was being punished for deciding to make a complaint, for challenging their complete power.

'You think you're clever, do you, complaining?' a couple of them asked me one day. 'You think you can beat the system? No one gives a fuck about you in here. You're going down for life, Howarth, because you're guilty. So you just carry on complaining.'

Even some of the other inmates warned me off. 'Stuart, don't complain,' they said. 'No one likes a complainer.'

One evening a couple of the screws came to my cell for a chat, pretending to be friendly, although I could see they had an ulterior motive. 'Why didn't you know what your dad was doing to you was wrong?' one of them asked, as if making casual conversation.

'What do you mean?'

'Well, why did you leave it till now to say something? Surely you must have known.'

'Why are we having this conversation?'

'Just intrigued by your case. You tell us you don't like strip-searches, why didn't you know that what your dad was doing was wrong?'

I could sense the antagonism in their voices. I could imagine the sort of things they'd been saying about me to one another, especially since I'd started making complaints about Smith. Some of the decent screws had told me they agreed with me and that he was a tosser, but there were a lot of them who didn't think any prisoner should ever have the right to complain about anything in

their treatment. There were some very good and fair officers in there, but they were the minority. The rest could
never resist the temptation to have a dig.

'Oh, Howarth, got anything you want to complain
about today, have yer?' was a greeting I got most days.

Mum had got in contact with a charity called One in
Four, which helped people who had been abused as kids.
The charity got its name from their belief that one in
four people have suffered some sort of abuse in their
childhood, which is a mind-blowing figure when you stop
to think about it. A guy called Colm O'Gorman came
from the charity to talk to me. He told me he would try
to get me moved; he could see I was losing my marbles
in Strangeways.

Sue and Geoff Hadfield, who had written to say how
sorry they were to hear about my troubles, came in to
see me, and asked if there was anything they could do
to help. They offered to put up bail, going to court
twice to try to push it through, even offering to have
me live in their own home with them, but both times
they were refused.

'On the evidence I have seen,' the judge at one of the
applications said, 'Stuart Howarth is a cold-blooded
killer. There is no way I will grant him bail.'

Christina was there, listening, and she started to cry.
'Get that woman out of my court,' the judge bawled and
a policeman went to grab her.

I hated him for talking to my sister like that and started crying and shouting at him, accusing him of being a paedophile, before stamping off, handcuffed, downstairs from the dock, with my guards following.

'Why in God's name did you call the judge a paedophile?' my barrister wanted to know.

'Why not?' I snapped, like a sulky child. 'He called me a cold-blooded killer. I'm not a danger to society.'

'If he ends up trying your case and you're found guilty you're going to be looking at a very long sentence.'

When things had calmed down a bit I was taken back upstairs. Christina was allowed to remain in court and the judge took his wig off, making himself seem a little more friendly. But I was bitterly disappointed that the hand of friendship that had been stretched out to me by the Hadfields had been torn away by a system that couldn't seem to understand what was happening to me and my family.

I felt an enormous love for Sue and Geoff, and in Geoff I was increasingly seeing a man whom I would love to have had as a father. He was willing to trust me and stand up for me, just as a father should for a child, regardless of what other people said I had done.

I was starting to bleed heavily from my rectum again, just as I had as a child. They took me to the hospital without any warning, double cuffed to a screw and driven in a minibus to have a camera inserted into my anus.

'You'll enjoy today, won't you,' one of the screws said, 'having things shoved up your arse?'

'Why do you have to keep making fucking remarks?' I wanted to know. I couldn't understand why men who were supposed to be in charge of my health and my rehabilitation would want to abuse me in almost the same way my dad had, exercising their power over me at every opportunity, taunting me, baiting me. I was an adult, not a kid; did I really have to accept it?

Before they could put the camera in the nurse told me they had to give me an enema to clear everything out of the bowel.

'Go ahead,' the screw who was attached to me said.

'There's no way you're staying here while that happens,' I said.

They handcuffed me to the bed while they inserted the tube. Once the enema took effect they unlocked the handcuffs and the screws went to the toilet with me. 'Go on, lad, push it all out,' they cheered as I emptied my bowels. For someone who had never been able to use a public toilet or do anything if there were other people close by it was a horrible ordeal and by the time we got to the room for the procedure I was crying.

Privacy while going to the toilet was always a problem for me in prison. There were some screws who seemed to linger excessively at the peephole in my cell door whenever I was trying to go. As a result I would try to get it over as quickly as possible, pushing and straining and causing damage, which would lead to bleeding and more anxiety. I'm sure it was part of the reason why I had end-ed up in hospital that day.

I was going to be sedated for the insertion of the cam-era and the screws wanted to be in there with me. The doctor could see how panic-stricken that was making me and seemed unhappy himself with their attitude.

'You don't have to be in here,' he insisted. 'There's only one door in and out of the room. I insist that you wait outside.'

It seemed that in life's great game doctors outranked prison guards when they were in their own hospitals and the screws grudgingly gave in and left. The doctors were very kind. They could see from my records that I had been through a lot. Once the procedure was over they told me that I had colitis, but that they could give me medication for it. Whenever people talked to me kindly, in gentle voices, I was unable to stop myself from crying. It reminded me of how I used to try to cuddle close to Mum for comfort after Dad had hurt me, when we went in the van to pick her up from work, or how I tried to create reasons for my teachers to take me on their laps.

All the way back to the prison the screws were making the same jokes and comments as I sat miserably in my cuffs. As soon as we got back I was strip-searched, even though they hadn't taken their eyes off me all day. I was then left sitting in the sweat room for three or four hours until they were ready to take me back to the wing, which meant I was too late to have any tea, even though I'd had nothing to eat all day because of the sedative I was given.

I was also too late to be allowed to make a phone call to Tracey. There was no comfort for me from anywhere as I curled up on my bed and tried to find some escape from the pangs of misery and hunger in sleep.

The next day they told me they'd lost yet another form that I'd used to make a complaint about the way they were treating me. Everything seemed to be conspiring against me. I felt helpless and suicidal.

During a phone call with Christina, she told me that someone had rung her house and threatened to do something to her kids unless she dropped her charges against the babysitter. I immediately started panicking and told the security officer I needed to talk to the police, to get her help.

'Howarth,' he sighed, 'go away. We're fed up with your fucking moaning.'

'Please,' I pleaded, 'I need to speak to the police.'

'I've told you, fucking go away. Go and sweep the stairs or something.'

'Fuck off!' I shouted, hurling my brush down like an angry kid.

'I'll fucking nick you for that!'

'Nick me. Fucking nick me. Go on, nick me.'

'I'll press the button.'

'Press the fucking button.'

He pressed the button, the alarm ripped through the wing, and the screws all started running about with their bunches of keys jangling and their boots cracking down on the walkways and stairs as everyone was put behind their doors like they were preparing for some sort of major riot. I found myself encircled with screws, all waiting for orders to restrain me.

'If you fucking touch me,' I warned, 'I'll hurt one of you. But if you leave me I'll walk.'

I started crying and one of them tried to take my arm.

'Fucking get off me!'

I was frogmarched off to a dark floor with cells all along one side. They put me into one, and one of the screws came up close to me. I could tell he was looking for trouble – he had the same air about him that Dad used to have when he was just looking for an excuse to batter me. The screw leaned forward until his forehead was against mine.

'You think you're fucking hard?' he shouted. 'You wanna kick off? Get on with it then.'

'If you're going to do me,' I said, looking round at them all, 'then do me. There's not a lot I can do about it, is there?'

'Get your fucking clothes off,' he ordered.

They strip-searched me then left me. I was now on the block, and I stayed there for four weeks in solitary confinement.

In solitary there was nothing to do all day but sit and think, remembering and reliving my past, over and over again. I was allowed to see my solicitors as normal, but if I got a visit from Tracey we had to talk through glass and we weren't allowed to touch. One time they wouldn't let her in because they said the dogs had sniffed her out as having drugs on her, which was ridiculous.

I kept trying to make complaints about victimization, because if I stopped trying I felt they would have won. I believed that everyone in the prison hated me, particularly the screws. There was one officer who had seen a picture of me in a local paper wearing a hard hat, who started calling me 'Bob the Builder'. I didn't mind the joke at first, but he started to sing whenever he was locking me into the cell: 'Bob the builder, Bob the builder', then he'd slam the door, flick up the flap and finish with, '... stick it up your arse!' Another officer would regularly call me a 'cocksucker', knowing full well about my past.

Chapter Eighteen

GUILTY OR NOT GUILTY

I went to court on 26 March 2001, charged with murder. The police resolutely refused to reduce it to manslaughter. I had no idea how things would go for me, but I was very unsure how I would be able to cope if I was given a life sentence in Strangeways. If I was found guilty of murder, I had decided I would hang myself with a sheet. And I dreaded walking into court and finding myself looking at the judge I had accused of being a paedophile, the same man who had said with such certainty that I was a 'cold-blooded killer'.

A doctor had given me a letter confirming I suffered from claustrophobia, so they took me to court in a car instead of a sweatbox. The screws wouldn't allow me to wear a suit and try to make myself look and feel more respectable; they said I had to wear a scruffy pair of jeans I'd been wearing for months because there are only certain times of year when you are allowed to send clothes in to Strangeways. They wouldn't even allow me to take a shower before I left.

When we got to the court my lawyers met me with the good news that we had a different judge, Mr Justice Elias, a man who was an expert in child abuse cases. They assumed he had been selected specially for the case. The prosecution then made me an offer. If I would plead guilty on the grounds of diminished responsibility, they would accept a ten-year sentence. There was no way I was going to admit guilt under any circumstances. If the whole story came out in court, I was sure they would see the truth. I didn't feel guilty. I didn't feel like it was my fault.

They then came back and offered me eight years in exchange for a plea of guilty to manslaughter. I wasn't willing to go for that either. I wanted a chance to speak up and be listened to, something that had never happened to me in the past. They came with another offer of five years.

'No,' I said, 'I'd rather go to trial.'

'But you'll go to trial on murder,' my solicitor Padhee said. 'You'll get a lot more than five years if they find you guilty. You've already served nine months, you could be out in two or three years.'

'I want the judge and jury to decide. I'm not guilty of what they're saying.' I was adamant.

There was so much toing and froing that the case didn't even get heard that day and I had to go back to Strangeways and return in the morning.

'We all talked about it last night and the prosecution is willing to leave it up to the judge to decide,' Padhee told me. It was a risk, but it seemed like one worth taking.

As we went up to the courtroom I was unsure quite what was going on. I wished I were dressed better. It seemed disrespectful to be standing in front of the judge in such a state. I was shaking uncontrollably.

'How do you plead, guilty or not guilty?'

'Not guilty to murder. Guilty of manslaughter due to diminished responsibility, in provocation and self-defence.'

The judge gave a short nod. 'I accept that this case be accepted as manslaughter on the grounds of diminished responsibility. But I don't accept provocation or self-defence. Sit down, Mr Howarth.'

I did so, listening while the prosecution read their case summary out. Then the defence read theirs. For the first time in my life I was hearing my story being spoken by other people. The pictures all came into my head and I couldn't contain my emotions. I knew my family were all in the room, although I couldn't see them because they were seated above me.

Years and years of pain and hurt bubbled to the surface and I wept uncontrollably. All the psychiatrists' and doctors' reports stated that I was truthful and that my stories could be substantiated by others. Even the police psychiatrist seemed to support my story, although he wrote it in a more critical style since he was part of the prosecution machine. The guards kept passing me tissues but I couldn't stop crying. The room went silent at one point and I turned to see what was happening. The security guard who had been passing me the tissues was now crying as well. I felt so relieved that people were finally hearing the truth, and I felt sure that my ordeal would soon be over. Now they all knew what I had been through they would understand how it had unbalanced my mind and made me lash out with the hammer when I thought I was going to be attacked again. They would never be able to sentence me to more years in jail now they understood. I just had to live through this last ordeal, this last humiliation of having my past laid out for everyone to stare at, and then I would be able to go home to my family and to Tracey, who was my whole world.

The newspapers were all sympathetic the next day, and Colm O'Gorman, from the child abuse charity, drummed up a lot more sympathy and support by speaking out for me.

When he had heard the whole case the judge told us that it was one of the most graphic cases he had ever come across and that Dad was a sick and twisted man. He agreed that the suffering we had all been through had been enormous. But irrespective of the victim's defects, his purpose as a judge was to serve justice and he still had to uphold the rule of law at all costs. He accepted that I was suffering from diminished responsibility and that I was not the master of my mind and could not be held responsible for my actions. He didn't accept provocation because if my mind were diminished, how would I know if I was being provoked? It had also been too long since the last time that I had seen Dad. He dismissed the self-defence idea for similar reasons. How would I have known if it was a perceived danger or a real one? He didn't know whether I took the hammer with me or not, but he didn't think that mattered if I was suffering from diminished responsibility. He decided, having taken everything into account, that I should be sentenced to two years in prison.

I couldn't understand what had gone on. There were too many words to take in when my emotions were running too high and jumbling up the messages on the way to my brain. All I wanted was to be with my family, but I'd been told they wouldn't be allowed to see me after sentencing. I was led away in a daze, trying to take it all in. One of the female security officers took pity on me and gave me a hug. Another guard asked if I wanted any crisps or a cup of tea. I didn't know what I wanted. I was relieved that I hadn't been found guilty of murder and sent down for life, but at the same time I could hardly bear to give up the hope I'd had that I would be walking free at the end of that day.

'You sit down,' the guard said. 'It's all right. You shouldn't even be in prison. I thought you'd be off home today, lad.'

I wished the staff at Strangeways could be as kind and understanding. I wished some of them could have been in court to hear my story and see the effect it had on people hearing it for the first time. I looked up as Padhee came in. He seemed to be moved as well and gave me a hug.

'You've changed my life, you know, Stuart,' he said. 'You've affected it deeply. Everyone's on your side and this decision today is the right decision. You've just got to go on and build your life now.'

My barrister came to see me and shook my hand.

'It was a good result,' he said. 'I think that judge was picked particularly for the job because of his background. There were political reasons because there has been so much paedophile activity in North Wales, with some high-profile cases in care homes. They were also worried that your stepfather had managed to get himself a job so easily and become friendly with the Mayor. I think there were some invisible hands at work behind the scenes on your behalf. I wish you the best of luck with your life.'

I did feel pleased that I had been vindicated and that people were accepting that these things do happen in life, but I was still shocked and bewildered. I felt empty, sad, lonely and desperate.

The door of the cell opened again and one of the guards was standing there. 'We're not really supposed to do this,' he said, 'but your friends and family from the court are here to see you.'

I started to cry again, but I felt frightened at the thought of seeing them all, not sure if I would be able to hold myself together. They directed me to a room, which had glass down the middle with all these friendly faces standing on the other side. As well as Tracey and Mum and Christina, Seb was there, and other friends from home, and Colm O'Gorman and Geoff Hadfield, all the people who had come to see me in prison and worked so hard for me on my case. As I walked in they all cheered and my tears welled up again. I dropped my head. I wasn't sure it was a day for cheering, even though I had been vindicated. It seemed a sad day. I had spent the day listening to my life being re-run, with all the pictures coming back into my mind, and I felt sorry that I had ended up taking another man's life. I was sorry I had taken Clare and Alex's dad and I wanted to apologize to them both face-to-face. I still haven't been able to do that with Alex, but when I did sit Clare down to tell her how sorry I was she didn't seem particularly interested in hearing it; she has other things on her mind, although none of us are able to know what they might be.

Tracey came up to the window and pressed her hand against it. I placed my palm against hers with the cold glass between us. The others all made their excuses and left the room, leaving us alone. We were both crying.

'It's over now, love,' I said. 'I just want to get on with my life.'

We talked for a while and then she said she had to go because they'd promised to talk to the television and radio people.

'I love you, Tracey,' I said.

'I love you too, Stuart.'

I watched as she left the room and then the guards came to take me back to the cell, reminding me that it wasn't quite over yet. There was a terrible pain deep

in my chest, which made me cry. I still longed for the
father I'd never had. I kept asking myself the same questions. How did I get here, and how could it have all come
to this?

I sat there for several hours before the prison officers
came down in their car from Strangeways to fetch me. It
was a surprisingly quiet ride back. By the time we
reached Strangeways the results of the case had already
been on the news.

'So, you're going home, are yer?' the officer at reception sneered. 'Not going yet though, are yer? You'll be
back. Now get yer clothes off.'

After the strip-search I was put back into the sweat
room for a few hours until there was someone free to
take me back to the wing. It didn't matter what I said or
did, they would never change their attitudes towards
me. 'Whatever, Howarth,' they would say with a world-
weary knowingness in their cruel voices. 'We've heard it
all before.'

As I walked on to E Wing I was aware that everyone
was looking at me. I could imagine what they were thinking. I was no longer one of them. They were all in for
years and I would be out within six months with remis-
sion and the time I had already served.

'Well done, Howie,' one of them said.

'Yeah. Well done, mate,' said another.

Even though they all came up to shake my hand and

tell me that I shouldn't be there, I could sense hostility in the air. I guess they were pleased for me, but many of them still had their trials to get through, and they knew they were unlikely to get off as lightly as me. A lot of them bombarded me with questions about what had happened in the courtroom, obviously trying to formulate a picture of what it was going to feel like when their own trial dates finally arrived. By about eight thirty I was back in the cell and the doors were being banged and locked all round the wing.

'Howie, you're on the telly!' a voice shouted.

I turned on the set and there was a picture of me as a boy on a slide. The voiceover was talking about how 'this sweet-natured little boy' was driven to kill his stepfather. Christina and Tracey came on, looking very nervous. The interviewer was making the point that men and boys are never listened to when it comes to things like rape and abuse, whereas women and girls now get fair hearings most of the time. They talked about how many men there must be out in the world who have been severely traumatized from things that have happened to them when they were young. Maybe, if someone had asked me if Dad had ever done things to me at the time he was arrested for interfering with the girls, I could have been given some counselling then that would have helped me to grow up and mature in the normal way, and would have saved Dad's life in the long run, but it just never occurred to anyone to ask. They even talked about the poor treatment I was receiving in Strangeways. Hearing my own story told as I lay in my cell made me cry all over again. I suddenly felt very low, wishing everything had been different in my life and I hadn't had to go through any of it. I felt embarrassed to think that everyone else on the wing was watching and listening to my life being talked about.

It felt as if I had only just managed to get off to sleep when it was morning again and the guards came round banging on the doors to wake us up. I was told to report to the office.

'Right, Howarth. Pack your bags. You're moving.'

'What do you mean?'

'You're moving to another wing. This isn't the right one for you; you're not a lifer, despite whatever we think. Go upstairs and pack your kit.'

Although I was relieved to be getting off that wing, it's still scary whenever you move cells because it means taking a leap into the unknown, meeting new people and getting to know new rules, finding out who can be trusted and who can't. As I sat waiting in my cell the other lads came by to shake my hand and wish me luck. I gave away a few things I'd accrued, like a crucifix and a poem.

I was escorted across to D Wing.

'You're Howarth, are yer?' the security officer greeted me.

'Yeah.'

'We're gonna have a bit of peace and quiet in here, are we?'

'What do you mean?'

'You like making complaints, don't you?'

'No. I try to treat people with respect and dignity and I'd like a little bit back.'

'Yeah, well you're an inmate.'

He pointed out where my cell was. As I packed up my kit and was about to set off to it I passed another lad.

'You've got a good cell, haven't you?' he said.

'What do you mean?'

'There's all the nonces there to keep you company.'

I suddenly realized where it was, right opposite A Wing, which housed all the sex offenders. I was only about thirty feet away from them. It felt like I was being punished again. They had selected me to go there in order to rub my nose in it. It might have been an accident, but after everything that had been said and done to me since arriving in Strangeways, it seemed a bit of a coincidence. When I got to the cell I realized I was sharing with another lad, who asked if I had any heroin the moment I walked in. People kept coming in and out of the cell and I was aware they were smoking heroin and other stuff.

I went back down to the office.

'Do I have to share a cell, boss?'

'We tell you what to do in here, Howarth.'

'I'm just frightened and I've got a lot of things going on in my mind ...'

They wouldn't listen. The next morning they didn't take me to get my anti-depressants, which worried me because the doctors always stressed that I shouldn't come off them suddenly in case it affected the balance of my mind, but they did eventually escort me over for a session with Neil.

'You're a bit late,' he said.

'They wouldn't bring me any earlier.'

He went outside and I could hear a bit of an argument going on. He came back in with a cup of coffee in a china cup, as he often did, and a guard asked to have a word.

'Inmates aren't allowed drinks in china mugs; they're for staff only. Don't you know inmates carry diseases?'

When we were finally able to sit and talk he told me he'd written a letter to the prison governor about the way they had been treating me.

'The governor called me before your trial and asked about these complaints you're making. "What's the problem with Howarth? Does he think he runs the jail?" I supported you on a few things, but she just said, "Howarth's a killer and he's charged with murder." I pointed out that that was for the court to decide, but she was worried that because you had got a single cell you would think you had won. She wanted to know why I had backed your request for one, so I explained how I believed it affected your condition. I said I was worried about your safety and your cellmate's if there was any perceived danger to you. Now they've all pretty much blackballed me, they won't talk to me, although I can see they're all talking about me behind my back. I'm beginning to feel a bit threatened myself and I think I may leave once you're out.'

He was horrified to hear I was back to sharing a cell and that I had been put so close to the sex offenders' wing and promised to have a word, although I knew that would not happen overnight.

I stayed in my cell for the next week or so, too frightened to go anywhere, constantly nervous of my cellmate and his friends but not having any alternative. It was another big wing of about two hundred prisoners and there was always an air of frantic activity, which I found it hard to adjust to after the relative quiet of the maximum-security wing. I felt constantly traumatized.

There was an established system whereby people who wanted to buy drugs had to get a member of their family to send money to a given address outside the prison. Once the money had arrived, the drugs would be passed over. It was all incredibly organized. It was also possible to get credit, but if you didn't pay up on time you would be beaten up. Sometimes suppliers would provide drugs on the promise that they would be repaid after the next visiting day.

You always knew when a consignment of drugs came in on a visit, transferred in a kiss with a loved one and swallowed or inserted rectally, because several men would descend on a cell simultaneously to collect. Sometimes, if someone were trying to buy time they would claim they'd swallowed the drugs and the people they owed them to would have to wait for them to come through. The creditors would be round that man's cell every day enquiring if the drugs had come through their bowels yet, and you would be able to sense their levels of frustration building as they became increasingly suspicious that they were being fed a line. Sometimes someone who was supposed to be bringing in drugs to a visit would fail to show up, leaving the inmate 'ghosted'.

There was one lad who confessed to me that he had been ghosted, although he didn't dare tell the people he owed the drugs to. I heard the shouting in his cell getting louder every day that he didn't produce the promised gear, and sometimes I would hear the sound of punches landing. On the third day one of his visitors came and asked me if I had a shampoo bottle so he could have a shower, which I didn't. I later discovered that five of them were actually using one to give the lad an enema to speed up the delivery of the drugs that he had told them were still in his bowels. The next day he was so badly beaten up he had to be taken to the hospital wing. There was a lot of blood in his cell.

So many kids came into prison clean and went out on drugs. Some would be strong enough to fight their fears and stand up for themselves; others would need drugs to help numb them.

The moment a newcomer arrived the vultures would try to take whatever he had. They would take his trainers, his jeans, whatever they could get off him, and they would try to get him on drugs, because drugs are currency.

There was one lad who came in for assault. I could see how frightened he was and I advised him that if he kept

himself to himself everything would be OK. The following day I was leaning on the balcony looking down and I
saw two drug dealers going into his cell. The next time
I saw him, a few days later, his eyes were glazed.

I only had to endure the shared cell for a couple of
days before they moved me back to E Wing, to the side
that wasn't maximum security, but was still for lifers. At
least this time I knew a few of the others and felt slightly
more comfortable as people greeted me like an old friend.
They put me in a relatively large and relatively clean cell,
on my own. I suddenly felt able to breathe again. They
asked if I would like to work on the servery. They'd been
having some trouble at meal times and wanted someone
big around who might calm things down. I knew they
were using me, but I didn't care if it was making my daily
life more bearable.

Because I wasn't having any luck with the complaints
and was still getting all the snide comments from
screws like Smith and the guy singing 'Bob the Builder',
I'd gone to a firm of solicitors in London with Colm
O'Gorman's help. A lawyer came to see me and I gave
him copies I'd made of every complaint form and all the
other details. His firm were specialists in dealing with
child abuse cases and he told me that the prison authorities would have to respond to my complaints within a
certain time limit. The authorities now knew that I was
serious about pursuing my rights, which may have made
them slightly more cautious of me, but it certainly didn't
help my popularity.

Since I didn't think my reputation with the authorities could sink any lower, I also put together a petition complaining about the conditions on the wings, like filthy bed sheets and towels that had to be used for washing ourselves and the lack of plastic feeding bowls. I complained about how some of us were being locked up all day with no exercise, how some of the sinks had no taps or no plugs. How we would eat in our cells but there was no means of disposing of left-over food at weekends, so it would stay rotting in the cells for days. If you put it down the toilet it would block it, so most lads threw it out the window for the ever-growing number of rats in the courtyard below. The rats mainly came out at night, like a rippling tide sweeping through all the detritus and rubbish. There didn't seem to be any proper hygiene policies, as there had been at Forest Bank and Altcourse, where litter was always being collected up in black plastic bags. I took the petition round and got about eighty people to sign it.

Although they were allowed to open prisoners' mail, they weren't allowed to open anything that was marked as coming from the prisoners' lawyers. They didn't even bother to hide the fact that they were flouting that rule in my case.

'Put in a complaint then,' the security officer suggested when I mentioned it. 'You're good at that, aren't you?'

One day when I got back to my cell I found that all my plastics had gone. I knew the rules; I could get nicked for losing them because they were my responsibility. I went to one of the screws.

'Boss, I've no plastics. Someone's had them off.'

'You must have thrown them away.'

'I've not thrown them away.'

'Well, what do you want me to do about it?'

'Well, I've got nothing to eat off. I need a bowl.'

'Leave it with me, I'll sort you out.'

He went down to the courtyard, where the rats and pigeons congregated, and picked up a bowl that had been standing on the ground under a drainpipe. He brought it back in and banged out all the mud and shit in front of me. It was scuffed and grimy with age.

'There you go,' he said, handing it to me.

'What am I meant to do with that?'

'You wanted a bowl. You've got one now.'

'You expect me to eat out of that? I wouldn't expect a dog to eat out of that.'

'I'm not asking a fucking dog to eat out of it,' he said. 'I'm asking you to. That's the only bowl you're getting. If you don't want it, give it back, but that's all you're getting.'

I took the bowl, knowing I had no option at that stage, and tried to scrub it as clean as I could. It was about a month before I was able to get a replacement off someone who was leaving. It was just like eating from the dog bowls Dad used to make us lick out.

Wherever I went, whenever I passed a screw, they had a smart-arse comment to make. It was like being the unpopular kid in a school playground where the bullies have been given free run to do whatever they please.

Whenever I had a visit it always meant I would have to spend a few hours in the sweat room on the way there or back, and I would be amongst lads I'd never met before, never knowing anything about them, often witnessing fights, always terrified. I was always the last to be let out. Now I was no longer in the maximum-security cells they didn't have to strip-search me each time unless they felt there was a good reason to suspect I was carrying something. Even though they had never ever found anything on me, they continued to single me out every time.

Smith often seemed to be on duty when I had visits. I would be able to feel his eyes piercing into my back.

'Is he looking at me?' I'd ask Tracey.

'Yeah, but don't worry about it.'

But I couldn't concentrate on the visit as long as I felt him prowling around behind me, looking for an excuse to have a go or make a remark. Sometimes a screw would just come up and stand right next to us, so we couldn't talk in private. It was very intimidating. When Tracey came in I would stand up to give her a hug.

'Fucking sit down, Howarth!'

If she got up to get herself a drink of water during the visit I would watch their eyes following her.

Knowing that they knew all my private business, I was soon aware that they were searching through my cell whenever I was away working in the servery, reading my diary. I would deliberately leave markers in it and find them moved when I got back. They weren't allowed to search a cell without the prisoner being present but they didn't care about that. What was I going to do about it? Make another complaint? All my mail was slowing down now, coming through already opened. The screws took pleasure in letting me know they knew my business before I did.

'How's Tracey doing in that job?' one would ask.

'You what?'

'Oh yeah, you haven't had that letter yet, have you?'

It seemed they just wanted to let me know that I couldn't put anything past them, that they were the ones in charge.

'It's your missus' birthday today, isn't it? How old is she? Forty? She doesn't look it, does she? She looks well for her age.'

Chapter Nineteen

PICTURES OF THE OUTSIDE WORLD

few weeks later I was on the move again because they needed my space for someone else, and I ended up in a cell on my own in B Wing. I knew a couple of the lads on there, which made the move easier.

I put in applications for home leave and for tagging, which meant I had to go and see one of the governors.

'Do you think you've been a good prisoner while you've been in here?' he asked.

'I think I've done my best, given the circumstances.'

'It's a very serious offence you've been convicted of. We don't think you are ready to go home on detention curfew.' He sat back and looked straight at me. 'Do you intend pursuing these complaints?'

'Well, yeah.'

'With all that's going on we don't think you should be going home on curfew.'

'This is a joke, isn't it? All you've brought me in here for is to see if I'll drop these complaints. Are you telling me that if I drop them I can have a tag?'

'It's nothing to do with the complaints.'

I knew there was no point arguing and asked to be taken back to the wing. I was determined not to be intimidated into withdrawing my complaints. It just didn't seem right that the people who were supposed to be rehabilitating me should be able to get away with abusing me further. If I didn't stand up for myself, what was to stop them going on doing it to other people? Someone had to say that enough was enough and things should change. I was desperate to get out of prison, since every hour in there reminded me of my childhood and I desperately missed Tracey every moment we were apart, but I wasn't willing to be blackmailed.

For the next few weeks I kept a low profile, just serving out my time. One of the hardest things about being in prison is not really being able to understand what is going on in the outside world, because you only see it through the newspapers and television. So when there was rioting in Oldham, around the area where Mum's pub was, I immediately feared the worst. Mum and Trevor lived right on the border between two areas, one of which was almost exclusively white and the other almost exclusively Asian. There had been trouble brewing for years, but it finally ignited and I saw television news pictures of the streets round the pub filled with angry mobs, riot police and burning cars. There were also some shots of a wrecked pub, although I knew it wasn't Mum's.

I was back on cleaning duties so I was able to get to a phone to call home and one of the cleaners at the pub picked up. I could hear strange noises in the background, like the sweeping up of broken glass.

'What's that noise?' I wanted to know.

'I don't know that I should tell you, love,' she said.

'What is it?' I insisted.

'The pub was attacked last night.'

I had a sudden vision of the wrecked pub I had seen on the news that morning and imagined Mum and Trevor standing in the middle of something similar.

'How's me mum? What happened?'

'Well, Clare was down in the bar last night helping to collect glasses. There were only a few people left and they were just getting ready to go and then bricks started flying through the windows. Clare was frightened and screaming and Trevor went to the door to see what was going on. There were hundreds of Asians outside, hurling these bricks. He got a pool cue in case they tried to come in while your mum phoned the police, and then he went back out to plead with them to go. Then one of the bricks hit him and they all started attacking him. Your mum tried to wade in and help him and she got punched.'

Picturing the scene was making me panic and I started to tremble.

'Are they all right?'

'Trevor's in hospital with a fractured skull, but your mum's all right, just a bit shaken up.'

I was crying and shaking as I put the phone down and turned round, coming face to face with two Asian guys.

'You bastards,' I shouted. 'This is your mob!' I knew they were from Oldham and in for riotous behaviour.

'What you fucking on about, mate?'

Everything was a bit of a haze after that, but I do remember getting into a fight with these two guys, the alarms going off and prison officers running around getting everyone into their cells. Once the wing was locked down they turned their attention to me and about twenty of them surrounded me. Usually at that point they get you down on the floor with a knee on your head and your arms twisted up your back, pinning you down until things have calmed. But for some reason they didn't pounce on me like that.

'Right, Howarth, you're gonna come quietly.'

I had no fight left in me. It had been an illogical outburst of fear and anger and it had passed now. I let them lead me down to the underground cells, knowing there was no point in protesting. I had been out of order and I was going to have to accept the consequences. I was going to have to serve time in the block.

'Get all your clothes off, except your underpants.'

I did as they ordered and then they locked me in, just as Dad had used to lock me naked in the cellar at Cranbrook Street. I sat on the mat, which was the only thing in the room, and waited.

'You're being charged with a racist attack,' the security officer told me when he eventually arrived. 'You'll stay down here until it's time for you to see the governor.'

The hours ground past and the boredom became excruciating. I found a piece of fluff on the floor and started flicking it around, just to give myself something to think about. Then I found a spider and played with that for a while, putting it on one side of the cell and counting how long it took for it to get to the other side, just waiting for someone to decide it was time for me to do something else. I had no idea what the time was or how long I had been in there. It was much quieter than being in the main block. I could hear the odd movements, but I couldn't work out what they were.

Suddenly there was a commotion outside and I pressed my eye to the tiny flap in the thick steel door. I saw a lad with his arms twisted up his back and his legs contorted. He was covered in blood and screaming as the officers battered him to the ground, and kept on kicking and punching.

'Leave him alone!' I shouted, banging on the door. 'Leave him alone!'

I heard them throwing him into a cell and slamming and locking the door. Then they left and the only sound was the lad banging on the inside of the locked door and crying. The screws said he got his injuries by hitting his head against the walls, but I had seen them laying into him. I realized I'd got off lightly. It seemed they beat up small guys more readily than big lads like me. They were cowards and they knew the smaller guys couldn't fight back, unlike me.

When I went to see the governor he sentenced me to twenty-eight days on the block and took away all my privileges, and I was given an extra thirty days on top of my sentence. It was disappointing, since I had been starting to count down the days till I would be home, and now I had to go back a month.

The only thing to alleviate the boredom was when they served food. I only knew that a meal time was close because I would start to get the same hunger pains I remembered from my childhood and I would sniff round the door like a dog, hoping to detect the scent of approaching food. When they opened the door I had to follow a yellow line to the serving hatch, and then follow the same line all the way back. If you veered off the line and just took the shortest route you would be reported again and be in even more trouble. I guess that could be where the expression 'toe the line' came from. They wouldn't let the next person out until I was back in my cell.

There was a guy in the cell next to me who must have been a long-termer, transferred from another prison. When they let him out he took no notice of the line and went straight to the serving hatch.

'Where the fuck do you think you're going?'

'To get my dinner.'

'Walk the fucking line.'

'No,' he said. 'Go and check your rulebook. We haven't had to walk the line for the last five years and I know because I've been inside the last fifteen years.'

Colm, Mum and others wrote to everyone they could think of asking if I could be moved to a category B prison. A question was even asked of a minister in the House of Commons, but he replied that I was considered too much of a risk and had to stay wherever the prison service decided to put me. How could I be that much of a risk if they were planning to release me into the community anyway in a few months' time?

Other prisoners warned me to be careful at night, in case they came to beat me up, but there wouldn't have been much I could do about it. I had trouble sleeping, expecting someone to come busting through the door at any moment. Even though I could now see the finishing post for my ordeal, I still lived in fear almost every hour of the day and night, just as I had done when I was a kid.

A month before I was due to be released I was given an appointment to see a probation officer. Her name was Pat. She explained that I was going to be released after serving only fourteen months on the understanding that I was going to be good and law abiding.

'You mustn't communicate with any known criminals,' she explained, 'and you have to come and see me at least once a week so we can see how things are going. I've read your case notes. Do you want to tell me a bit more about yourself?'

She seemed a kind woman and so I started telling the story of Dad and my sisters.

'He was our stepdad actually, at least I think he was, but he adopted us.'

'You were adopted?' She looked startled. 'Where were you adopted?'

'Ashton Magistrates' Court.'

'And this was the man who abused you and who you killed?'

'Yeah, there was me and my two sisters, one of whom, Shirley, was in a wheelchair, but even that didn't stop him.'

She had fallen silent and I looked up to see if she was all right and whether she wanted me to go on talking. She had her hand over her mouth and her eyes were wide with shock. I felt suddenly frightened. Was it something I'd said?

'What's the matter?' I asked. 'Are you OK?'

She took her hand away from her mouth and spoke very slowly and deliberately as if trying to piece something together in her head as she went. 'I have a terrible feeling I was the one who dealt with your adoption. I was a magistrate in charge of adoption matters at the time. I remember the case because I remember your sister in the wheelchair.'

'There were three of you there,' I said and she nodded. 'And when you asked if I liked my new daddy I said I didn't like it when he hurt me, but I was frightened of upsetting him so I laughed.'

Her hand had gone back over her mouth and she was shaking her head from side to side in horror. She must have felt bad to think that she could have done something to save us at that stage, but in fact there was no way she could have known what was going on behind the façade that Mum and Dad put up that day. In fact he must have looked like a very noble man, willing to take on three children, one of whom was so severely disabled. Pat was always very nice to me after that and I never found it in my heart to bear her any ill will. There were plenty of other people along the way who could have guessed what was going on behind our closed family doors but never did. If even my own mother didn't realize I was being sexually abused, what chance was there that a stranger would have picked up on it?

'These sorts of things wouldn't happen today,' she kept saying to me, although I was never convinced by that – you only have to read the papers to see that they still do.

Geoff Hadfield came in to see me a few times and he kept saying things like, 'You're a grand lad; I'd have you as me son any day.' His words meant a great deal to me, as I would happily have had him as my dad.

'I knew the first day I saw you,' he said, 'that you had something special inside you. I'm not talking about friendship or anything like that, but the way you conducted yourself in business impressed me. I have been so shocked by what I've found out about you.'

Talking to him would upset me because it made me wonder why I couldn't have had a dad like him, someone who would have praised and encouraged me and told me that I was a great lad.

I was looking forward to having some in-depth counselling once I was out of prison to try to help with some
of the issues that were still making life seem so hard.
Apart from my sessions with Neil, I never received any
help or support from within the prison, and even when it
came time for me to leave there was no action plan.
There were no doctor's appointments, exit strategy,
counselling or even any thoughts as to how I would come
to terms with what I had done, let alone the abuse I had
suffered which had led to it. Prison was lock down and
then they kick you out. They didn't see it as their job to
worry about me when I was gone: that was somebody
else's problem.

My overwhelming desire was to be a good boy, a
good person, to be normal like everyone else. I also
wanted to help other people who had been through similar experiences. I knew I was one of the lucky ones
because I had been given the strength to survive everything that had happened to me and to try to fight for a
fairer deal in life. I knew most people who suffered from
abuse never managed to get that far. If any one of my
failed suicide attempts had worked I would just have
been one more statistic, one more of the many casualties
of childhood abuse.

There is so much ignorance still in the world about
the damage that happens to a child when they are physically, mentally or sexually abused. When I heard about a
little girl who had been tortured to death by her uncle
and aunt and someone on the television wondered why

she didn't tell anyone what was happening to her, I couldn't help myself from shouting at the screen: 'Because she didn't know that it was wrong. She didn't realize that everyone else's life wasn't like hers!'

We need to educate children and teach them about inappropriate behaviour in schools, as part of their sex education. It's no good telling children 'Don't talk to strangers', because most victims of abuse know the perpetrators well. Most abusers are within families or in positions of trust, so the child doesn't recognize that what they are doing is wrong.

The closer it came to my release date in September the slower the days seemed to pass as the rest of the world moved on without us. Inside Strangeways we heard about the destruction of the World Trade Center towers at the same time as everyone else who was watching television, and a sort of shocked hush fell over the prison that day. Sometimes outside events seem even more shocking when you are locked away because you have more time to think about them, and your imagination builds up terrible pictures of what might be happening. People on the outside could see that normal life was continuing all over the world, even though the political landscape had been changed forever, but we couldn't see that, we just saw the media pictures of the crashing planes and the falling towers.

The countdown to 19 September was unbearable, and the day itself started like every other prison day, the same jangling of keys, banging of doors and harsh shouts. I hardly dared to believe that I was finally going to be walking free, terrified in case someone in authority changed their mind and they locked me back up again. I was excited, but nervous about how the outside world would respond to me now that they all knew what I had done, and what had been done to me as a child. Would they see me as a 'cold-blooded killer', like the bail judge and like many of the prison staff? Would they see me as a bad boy who deserved his punishment, both as a child and as an adult? Or would they sympathize with me, like the people who had been forced to listen to my entire story in court?

I was escorted across to reception with the people who were going to court that day, so the screws didn't have to make more than one trip from the wing. We then met up with men from other wings who were being released or going to court. It was a pleasant late summer's day as we all sat together, waiting to be processed. Even at this late stage they wanted to keep us hanging around, to remind us that they were still in charge of our lives, if only for a few more hours.

I sat quietly, listening to the conversations going on around me. The ones who were going out were all discussing where they were going to score some heroin. I wondered how many of them had developed the habit since being inside Strangeways. Drugs had been so freely available, much more freely available than they are on the street, and there never seemed to be any effort to help users to rehabilitate.

Before I could be released they had to strip-search me one more time, just to remind me I wasn't a free man yet, that they could still terrorize me if they chose to. They then kept me in the sweat room for another two hours before finally letting me out through the big steel gates into the daylight.

It was such a wonderful feeling and I just wanted to make a new start, find out who I really was and get on with my life. As the gate slid back behind me I saw Tracey's red car and the picture was shot into a million pieces as my eyes filled with tears. As I walked towards the car it felt like my heart hit my stomach. Tracey got out and hugged me, but I was unsure how to respond, too filled with mixed emotions, still standing in the shadow of those towering brick walls. My shoulders began to jerk up and down and I sobbed uncontrollably.

I loaded my bag into the boot of the car just as Mum and Trevor drove up. Both of them got out and hugged me too. I was very conscious of the buses roaring past and all the buzz of normal life and I felt a tremor of panic at the enormity of taking charge of my own life once more. Was I actually up to the job?

'I just want to get out of here,' I said.

I climbed into the front of the car next to Tracey. 'I wouldn't be here if it weren't for you,' I told her. On the journey home I had to touch and hold her just as I had with Mum all those years ago, but my head was still bowed like that of a naughty child.

I turned and watched Strangeways disappearing as we drew away, a vile, hidden world filled with failure, ignorance, bullying and cruelty, like a lost community, isolated from all the warmth and kindness of the world outside. I shivered. I wanted to get away from it, but I was frightened of the thought of freedom. I wanted to hide in the comfort of my own room at home, in my own space, where it would be peaceful and safe away from life and other people.

'I love you,' Tracey said as she drove into the traffic stream.

'I know. Let's just get home.'

The bustle of the city outside the car was threatening to overwhelm me and I just wanted to get to the safety of Mum's pub as quickly as possible. When we got back I went straight to my room and sat down, just as I would have done if I were returning to my cell. It was what I was used to doing, what made me feel safe. Tracey came in and sat beside me, giving me a kiss. I remained tense and unresponsive. I might be out of Strangeways, but jail wasn't yet out of me. I had so many issues I was going to have to face before I could hope to lead a normal, happy life and I wasn't sure how I was going to deal with them unsupported.

My new journey was about to begin. I had to grow up from being the little boy I once was and I had to find Stuart, the man I really was!

Chapter Twenty

A NEW FATHER FIGURE

We had issued proceedings against Strangeways, and there was also the case against the babysitter coming up, so I knew I wasn't going to be able to put all my unpleasant experiences behind me just because Dad was gone and I was out of jail. I would have to relive them many times for the lawyers and the courts in order to let people know what was going wrong with our childcare and prison systems. It would have been nice to have forgotten about everything, but I knew that things would only get better if people like me spoke out about what they had seen and experienced.

'Are you sure you're all right?' Tracey kept asking in the hours after I was released. She must have expected me to be overjoyed at being out, eager to see everyone and embrace life, but I didn't really want to leave my room. I was in a state of shock, very like the night I came back from Dad's house in Wales. So many things frightened me, such as noises I would never have noticed before. For instance Tracey had a habit of shaking her car keys when she was about to go out, making them jangle. 'You're not a screw!' I would shout, unable to bear the noise.

I became meticulous about cleaning myself and my surroundings, sure that I could detect the smell of jail and determined to eradicate it. I needed constant reassurance that people liked me and didn't think I was a bad person because of what they had learned about me. My mind was going round and round in circles and I knew I was driving Tracey mad, but I couldn't help myself.

When Geoff Hadfield phoned I burst into tears as I thanked him for all he'd done.

'I'd like to see you tomorrow,' he said in his usual gruff, no-nonsense manner. 'Would you come down to the office?'

I was always happy to go and see the Hadfields, confident that their high opinion of me was genuine, that they believed I was a good person. When I got there Geoff took me up to the boardroom and Sue, who was also the Company Secretary, was already there, along with Maurice, their General Manager, and Paul, their Finance Manager. I was shocked and unsure what was going on or what they were expecting of me.

'Thanks for coming to see us today,' Geoff said, as if it were me doing him a favour rather than the other way round. 'I've had a talk amongst my colleagues. We've all worked with you before and we have a vacancy for a business development manager. We want you to do it.'

'Geoff,' I said, unable to stop the tears that were always so close to the surface from breaking through, 'don't feel sorry for me. I appreciate everything you've done because I've never had a father in my life, as you know. But I can't take charity, Geoff.'

'Look, pal,' he said, sounding mildly irritated at not getting the response he wanted. 'I might have a heart but I'm not an idiot. The reason I'm successful in my business is because of the commercial decisions I've made. The first time you came here I told you you should come and work for me. I saw something in you. You put us all at ease, you were professional, you looked the part, and I've not changed my opinion since then. I think you can bring something to our party here. You've worked with big businesses and you've had your own business. This is not about anything personal, Stuart. If you turn round and tell me you don't want the job that won't be a problem, but I'm offering you something commercial here, not personal. You'll always be my friend and I'll always be here for you, whatever you decide.'

His words made me cry even more. There I was, one day out of Strangeways, one day away from living in hell, being offered all I'd ever wanted by a man who was like a father to me. Coupled with Tracey, and Colm O'Gorman and Neil, I was finally beginning to see some good in the world, some reason to keep going and not keep thinking about ending it all.

I wanted that job more than anything, but I couldn't accept charity and I told him so.

'Will you do me a favour?' Geoff asked. 'Will you just do us a presentation on what you think the job needs and what you would do if you were to take it?'

'I owe you that much,' I said. 'But I'm still not accepting charity.'

The following week I was back at the office making a presentation on how I would handle the job if I had it, increasing the volume of wood on the site by fifteen thousand tons a year. I had done my homework meticulously, just as I always did when I was after a job or a contract. It was a good presentation and I knew it. When I'd finished they all applauded and Geoff started talking again.

'Right,' he said, 'I'm officially offering you the job.' He went on to detail exactly what he was offering in the way of pay, even the sort of company car he was willing to give me. Over the next few months he and the rest of his family gradually wore down my resistance and convinced me that it was a completely genuine offer. As I grew more accustomed to the outside world, I eventually felt sufficiently confident of my own abilities to give in and accept the job. It felt like I was joining a new family, a family where no one was frightened to express their feelings to one another.

There are so many people I need to say sorry to. To start with there are all the relationships that I made so impossible over the years because of how disturbed my mind was.

I'm sorry that I ended up taking a man's life and depriving his family of him.

I am really sorry for all the years of my children's early lives that I missed. I made contact with Matthew and Rebecca after I came out of prison and started to build a new relationship with them, starting by just going round to their house once a week and spending half an hour chatting to them at the door, trying to win their confidence back. Angela has done a great job of bringing them up and I'm sorry I wasn't able to be more help to her. Rebecca was thirteen years old when I finally got to go out with her. I felt like the proudest man alive as I walked around the shops of Oldham with her, but I was also aware that I would never now get to push her on the swings or take her to the park, or see her doing things at school events. I have to accept that both the kids think of Angela's current partner as their dad. They refer to me as their 'old dad', and I have to be content with that, even though it hurts. They changed their names to his even before I went to prison, because they wanted to be part of a proper family unit I guess, and I can understand that, but that hurts too. I am aware that they might not have turned out so well if I had stayed with them because I was very ill. They are both so beautiful and undamaged and I am very grateful for that.

For everything that went wrong in my life there was only one person I felt I could blame, and that was Dad, but there is also the system, which often listens but fails to act.

I now know for sure that David Howarth was my step-dad, just as he was for Shirley and Christina. Christina showed me a picture she had got from Mum of all of us posing as a family together. I am a baby, sitting on George Heywood's knee. I wish Mum had shown me that picture when I was a child, then at least I would have had a better idea who I was. I went to visit George. He's old now and suffering from dementia. I was surprised by how small he was. I felt no bond between us. He did not fulfil any of the needs or yearnings I had to find a father figure – that role has now been more than fulfilled by Geoff.

At his trial, the babysitter who had abused me and Christina was not convicted, partly because I was so nervous and unstable from my prison experiences that I made a very bad witness.

The case against Strangeways, however, was completely successful. The judge agreed that I had been abused and that the system was entirely unsatisfactory. Lord Justice Moses, who had just been overseeing the tragic Soham murders case, told me he didn't know how I stopped myself from punching Smith on the nose when he made his comments about me enjoying being abused. He found that many of the officers were lying about the way in which I was treated, that there was a severe lack of training in the prison service and that they had been performing the strip-search incorrectly. He said there was no doubt that I'd had my human rights infringed.

The judge ruled that the prison officers had caused a 'limited and temporary' exacerbation of my Post Traumatic Stress Disorder and said I should also be compensated for 'humiliation and loss of dignity', and he awarded exemplary damages after finding there had been 'misfeasance in public office', which referred particularly to Prison Officer Smith.

The judge did also admit that I probably was very annoying, the way in which I was writing everything down in my diary, but that at the same time I wasn't being given the correct medical care. Smith was dismissed from the service and I was awarded damages. The money was not important; what was important was that finally the world was listening to me and believing the things that I told them.

I learned the same day, however, that Smith had been reinstated, on the grounds that the prison service had not dealt with his disciplinary procedure correctly and within agreed timescales. This saddened and angered me and it seemed as though the prison service was having one last jibe at me. I was also concerned that he would be back on the wings and in the strip-search areas, free to dish out more punishment and abuse to other prisoners.

As I embarked on the long journey ahead I was so grateful for all the love and comfort I was being shown. The greatest gift in my life, Tracey, was still by my side, having proved her love to me without question. Now, I felt it was time to repay her loyalty and to build on the love we shared.

I hope that readers who have been brave enough to read to the end of my story will feel that, despite all the unhappiness and pain, there is still a message of hope. The children of dysfunctional families will always be damaged, but with the right help from caring and loving people, we can move on to live good and productive lives – we can even learn to love and to allow ourselves to be loved in return.